SEATTLE PEACE-MEAL DIET
a seduction into cruelty-free living

by the PAWS
Resource Book Committee

Illustrations by Cheryl Platt

printed by
George Banta Co.
Menasha, WI

This book was written by volunteers.
All profits will go toward local efforts to help animals and for
public education on animal issues.

Special thanks
in preparation of this book go to
Ira Sacharoff, Chris Suksdorf, Carla Elder, Karen and Les Kinney,
Virginia Knouse, Marjorie Spiegel, Bonnie Jean Steward,
Elaine Thorson, Bette Browne, Thelma Norian and Kim Weimer

© 1986 Progressive Animal Welfare Society
  P.O. Box 1037
  Lynnwood, WA 98046

ISBN 0-932649-00-9

*This book is dedicated especially to those
newly turning to animal issues who want the world to change,
and who are willing to take the steps —
starting most importantly in their own lives —
to make it change.*

TABLE OF CONTENTS

I refuse to eat animals because I cannot nourish myself by the sufferings and by the death of other creatures. I refuse to do so, because I suffered so painfully myself that I can feel the pains of others by recalling my own sufferings.

I feel happy, nobody persecutes me; why should I persecute other beings or cause them to be persecuted?

I feel happy, I am no prisoner, I am free; why should I cause other creatures to be made prisoners and thrown into jail?

I feel happy, nobody harms me; why should I harm other creatures or have them harmed?

I feel happy, nobody wounds me; nobody kills me; why should I wound or kill other creatures or cause them to be wounded or killed for my pleasure and convenience?

I think that men will be killed and tortured as long as animals are killed and tortured. So long there will be wars too. Because killing must be trained and perfected on smaller objects, morally and technically.

— Edgar Kupfer-Koberwitz
written while in Dachau
concentration camp

Seattle Peace-Meal Diet

There are several reasons people choose from when adopting a vegetarian lifestyle. The news these days is that in a world full of chemicals and diet-related disease, the average vegetarian suffers less deterioration than the average meat eater. Vegetarianism is the alternative diet that puts less stress on the environment; and if adopted by Americans, could probably lead to a great lessening of the hunger problem in our world. That, of course, is all good, but the perspective we will present in this book is of another side of vegetarianism that has not been represented fully enough in other meatless cookbooks, and this is vegetarianism from the animal rights point of view. Though the high consumptive meat diet is oppressive to the earth and to poorer humans around the world, the institution of meat eating most assuredly and directly oppresses the animals, whose total worth is calculated only according to how well they can be turned into dinner. It is to the animals then, that we would like to direct your concern.

So it follows — the purpose of this book is to provide information and resources useful to those people interested in "ethical" vegetarianism and cruelty-free living. Inside, you will find information about cosmetics, household products, and foods that in some way use animals in the process of their production. You will also find lists of alternative products and where to buy them in the Seattle area, as well as tips about restaurants and co-ops.

The recipes themselves have been collected from people throughout the Seattle area, and include both vegetarian and "vegan" offerings. If a recipe is vegan, it has an asterisk before the title signifying that no animal products (this means dairy and eggs as well as meat) are included in it. Some sections such as desserts and breakfasts are entirely vegan because we reasoned that a vegetarian cake recipe is easily found elsewhere . . . but a cake without eggs or milk?

Not *all* of our recipes are vegan, because though we feel the modern dairy and egg industries are, among other things, responsible for some of the most inexcusable confinement conditions, we realize that vegetarianism and self-education often come in steps. Any step away from the habit of eating/exploiting animals is a step we would like to congratulate you for taking.

We hope you will try the vegan recipes as well as experiment on your own. People often ask the vegetarian, "What can you eat?" Remember

1

that while there are basically only five meats the traditional meal is centered around, there are literally hundreds of usually unexplored vegetables and grains waiting for your discovery. Discover the alternative diet — a diet as simple or complicated, healthy or sinful as what you crave and are used to — and enjoy it in good conscience.

PAWS Animal Rights Action Committee
Recipe Book Committee

Leanne Clarke
Haley Land
Peggy Hanson
Jennifer White
Shirley Christensen
Chris Turner

How Farm Animals are Raised in the U.S.A.

Remember this old ditty?

Old MacDonald had a farm, and on this farm he had:

- *80,000 laying hens, four to a 12" by 18" cage, stacked and lined up, row after row, beaks removed, defecating on the caged hens below, living in artificial daylight to maximize their egg production to the point where they are no longer productive and they are slaughtered, or 'til they collapse from soft bones due to mineral depletion from making eggs.*

- *Female pigs, isolated in narrow stalls or tied down for as along as five years, consequently suffering from obesity and arthritis; all so that they won't fight among themselves in the forced, overcrowded pens.*

- *Veal calves raised in total confinement, often in total darkness, purposely fed an iron-deficient diet to give their meat its light color.*

- *A sterile, automated building, designed with artificial night and day, slatted floors that cause lameness, hormones and antibiotics whether they need them or not, social isolation, and no escape.*

- *So many animals that it was impossible, not to mention inefficient, to attend to or notice when a few were sick and dying while the majority were maintained.*

ee-i-ee-i-oo . . .

Readers, shake hands with the modern world. The farm conditions above are but the thinnest tip of the iceberg. The barnyards of your memories, your school readers, and your Sunday drives into the country today supply only a small fraction of our animal products. Most everything coming to cities like Seattle and their suburbs is raised where we can't see it, inside of buildings on the modern farm. The modern animal-raiser is not mean-spirited, but his or her animals are raised dispassionately. Animals are kept behind closed and locked doors; in part, so that conditions remain sanitary, but also so that the public won't feel anger and guilt. In this book, we hope to open those doors and give you a chance to make informed personal choices.

If you buy beef, pork, chickens, turkeys, rabbits, eggs or dairy products from Seattle-area supermarkets, you should assume the products you are eating were raised in a "factory." Not only are most of America's farm animals kept indoors, they are often totally confined in individual spaces the size of their bodies to save money and restrict movement that reduces their body weight. The confinement may last their entire lives. This system of intensively raising animals in little space, while denying normal

3

movement, socialization and instinctual drives, is known as factory farming. It is so dramatically the opposite of our *perception* of life for the farm animal, and it has only developed in our lifetimes. Indeed, it is one of the twentieth-century's best-kept secrets, and one of science's and agriculture's greatest lapses of conscience.

To have a factory farm, you begin with the premise that it is okay to treat an animal as an object, a commodity, a machine. The logic this allows, now that you've overcome your feelings about the farm animal's capacity for pain and pleasure, is that more animals crowded into less space is better. Better because it is more productive, which means more trips to the bank. A change from this brutal direction will come only when individual consumers change and begin choosing ethics over convenience and economy.

Farmers who will discuss ethics argue that animals are "happier" today because food, shelter and warmth are unvaryingly at the animal's disposal; and therefore, conditions now are actually more humane. All we ask of these farmers is to give their animals a choice and see whether chickens will volunteer to have their upper beaks sliced off, or whether pigs will wait in line to catch and mangle their feet on slatted floors, or whether veal calves will pay cash money to stay away from their mothers to eat a low-iron, anemic diet, or whether any of them will build their own cages because they have discovered how much happier they are, protected from the evils of moving about and socializing.

If every one of our slaughterhouses were constructed of glass, this would be a nation of vegetarians.

— Mel Morse
President of the Humane Society
of the United States

Our wish is to have you share our outrage. The factory farm, the place where most of America's and Seattle's meat, milk and eggs come from, does not respect the beings it uses. It denies space, light, and companionship; and it greatly increases an animal's stress and boredom. Farm animals are being coerced beyond their limits. It bears repeating that the public does not see the suffering because the majority of America's *four billion* farm animals raised annually are indoors and out of view, and the trend is increasing.

Not killing animals is generally seen as the motive behind ethical vegetarianism, but with today's farms, suffering is at *least* as important an issue as killing animals. We grew up on tradition and history which rejected animal cruelty — but for farm animals of today, cruelty is being called progress, and it is being systematically perpetuated in the buildings that have replaced the barnyard. There is a hole in our fabric of compassion. Whatever dominion some people believe we have over animals can only be wrong, badly wrong, when it is indifferent to an animal's pleasure and pain, and it is without conscience.

Clearly, vegetarianism is the most peaceful lifestyle we can choose. It causes far less suffering, and it is more consistent and in greater harmony with all life than other lifestyles. We strongly urge everyone to face up to this truth and change old habits. However, if you do not intend to become a vegetarian, you can take one step away from the cruelty of the factory farm. Refuse to buy animals and their products from supermarkets or anywhere else unless there is some proof the animal was raised with respect. Ethical vegetarianism is a change in lifestyle most of us would rather not confront; but we must remember, as we are taking something from animals, something is always owed in return.

"CONFINEMENT? YOU BET CONFINEMENT IS A PROBLEM. WE CAN'T SEEM TO EVER GET AWAY."

The Dairy Industry:
Spilt Milk Worth Crying Over

Question: What has four legs, udders, chews its cud and says, "RRmmm-RRRmmm-whrrrrrrrrrrrr?"

Answer: A cow — the American milking-machine.

Milk. You've heard that "it looks good on you," that it is "nature's most perfect food." What you *never* hear is how milk is obtained, and that's because sales would drop if the public knew that contented cows have gone the way of the hayloft and milk stool.

Dairy animals are among the victims of modern agriculture; however, unlike chickens and pigs, dairy cows — just by being dairy cows — have been mildly fortunate in being able to confound some of factory farming's most heartless confinement. This is only part of their story though. How long this decency may last will, in part, depend on public awareness and consumer responsibility; for agribusiness would be delighted to control dairy cows more intensively should the means become available, and if we were willing to buy the product.

And why shouldn't we? What happens to these cows that is so awful? You drive by a herd of them every morning on the way to the city. You know enough to even be sure they are a breed of dairy cows and not beef cattle. They don't look unhappy to you...

Fair enough. The cows you see might be okay. They moo and get a drink down by the stream. They swat flies with their tails and look after their newlyborn —

The calves? Where are the calves?

Life is not as without-a-care as it seems down on the farm. When only a few days old, the female and male calves are taken away from their mothers. If female, they may be raised as part of the herd, but fed from a pail. If male, they are marketed as quickly as possible. Some will become full-grown and then be slaughtered. A terribly unlucky number though, will be raised in a tiny, dark hell for three and a half months and then will be slaughtered as veal calves. More on this later.

Actually, you should have guessed by now that we are not going to let you get off so easy with your image of the dairy cows. First, look again. Are you sure the cows aren't beef cattle? Just because a cow has a set of udders doesn't mean anything, except that it is a female. In truth, some of those cows you have been driving past are the "property" of the meat industry. It is only the specially-bred, high-milk-output cows, like Guernseys and Jerseys, that are dairy cows. And as technology "advances," we can drive past fewer and fewer of the sum total that exist in the U.S. Today, approximately 50% of our dairy cows are confined and invisible.

Green pastures are being replaced by automatic feeding; open skies replaced by stalls, neck chains and holding barns. Most dairy cows now spend their time waiting. Waiting for the twice-daily milking routine. Time in-between is spent in confinement ranging from crowded pens to individual stalls to "tie-in" stalls, where the milking equipment is brought to the cow and the cow stays in the stall for months on end, chained by the neck. Confined dairy cows are on concrete or slatted floors. Their legs and hooves are not designed for this and they suffer foot injuries and constant pain.

The animals you call domestic need freedom too. You chain them up, day and night; you put them in narrow stalls, in dark and dirty stables. You kill their intelligence and soul-life by making them stare all their life at a wall, or a manger — and then, filled with contempt, you call them stupid!

— Author Unknown

The problems of building design may only impact half of our dairy cows, but attitudes within the dairy industry, particularly the willingness to view cows as production objects, affect the entire dairy cow population.

As they do with chickens, pigs, sheep and other domestic farm animals, farmers and business people want more and more from their investment. The cow, therefore, must be kept constantly pregnant so her milk supply will not dry up. Whatever maternal instincts she has are thwarted, since her calves are taken away from her just a few days after birth. She is intensively milked. Udder inflammation is often the result. She is genetically crafted to be a superproducer. Her udders and "milk bag" can be so abnormally huge that the weight of the five to six gallons of milk she is carrying drags close to the ground and she has difficulty even moving. But all of this contributes to greater profit, so rather than confronting her pain, boredom and discomfort, the farmer sees that she is given stimulants, chemicals and hormones to further increase her production. This usually goes on for five to six years, or until her production falls below three gallons per milking. At that time she is, of course, slaughtered. Her natural lifespan would otherwise be ten to fifteen years.

If you are like the average urban/suburban dweller, much of the above is news to you. It may be, however, that the plight of the dairy cow's male offspring, the veal calf, has reached your attention because of the recent public scrutiny of the veal industry.

Veal calves are primarily born to dairy cows. Like all calves, they are taken from their mothers a few days after birth. Not only are they not allowed to suckle — something they are driven by instinct to do — but they are fed, by pail, "milk replacer" made of reconstituted skim milk and whey, starch, fats, sweeteners, mold inhibitors and antibiotics.

People buy veal because it is fancy, tender and easy to digest. Very simply, it is special. Of course this means veal calves get special treatment, right? You bet it does. That tender meat is due to baby calves being *specially* placed in crates or in stalls where they cannot turn around and develop muscle tone. Muscle tone is not good tasting and tender. Being *specially* chained at the neck to further restrict movement also makes meat tender. Veal's milky-pale color is due to a *special* diet that is intentionally iron-deficient. It may make the calves weak and anemic, but milky-colored flesh is important. It does not matter that the color has nothing to do with how veal tastes. It gives veal that veal look. Farmers take *special* pains to keep their veal calves anemic. The calves are not even allowed straw floors because the iron-craving calves will eat it since there is iron in the straw. Instead, they get *special* hard, bare floors. Another *special* treatment of veal calves is the 20 to 22 hours of darkness they live in every day to keep their physical movements to a minimum, so that, once again, their muscles will not develop. This total darkness, ultimate confinement and cruel diet lasts for a uniquely *special* fifteen weeks. By this time, the calves are so anemic and neurotic they are slaughtered lest a higher percentage of them sicken and die and profits are not maximized. Yes, veal is very special. And remember . . . it comes from "contented" dairy cows.

Dairy production. Veal production. That is the picture we see today if we open those closed doors in the dairy businesses. The Seattle area is not

---

This is dreadful! Not (only) the suffering and death of animals, but that man suppresses in himself, unnecessarily, the highest spiritual capacity — that of sympathy and pity towards living creatures like himself — and by violating his own feelings becomes cruel.

— Leo Tolstoy

---

much different than the rest of the nation. The Puget Sound-area supermarkets buy milk, butter, cheese, cream, yogurt, etc. from the few wholesalers in the region, like Darigold®, who have in turn usually bought their dairy products from the Northwest Dairymen's Association, which buys from a collection of individual dairy farms. Some are less restrictive than others, but all make enormous demands of their cows, and frankly, it is hard to recommend one operation over another, knowing the cows are constantly pregnant and overproducing and that their offspring will be victimized at a very early age.

We are sorry to say finding a completely acceptable dairy farm will not be easy. We have not found one in this area. The milking equipment is so expensive. It is also nearly impossible to not market the cow's male offspring, or to keep the milking cow after she cannot reach minimum milk-production levels, and still be price-competitive with other dairies. But there are variables within the farms we have been describing, so if you want to visit any local dairy, in spite of certain givens, these questions should be asked:

1. Do the cows graze every day?
2. Are the cows ever chained up? If so, for how long? (This is only acceptable during milking.)
3. How much time are the cows forced to spend on concrete or slatted floors? (This too, is only acceptable during milking.)
4. Are the calves ever sold to veal farmers?

After reading about conditions on today's dairy farms, you might feel a visit is totally unnecessary, because you no longer want dairy products in your life. If you feel that conviction, it does much to fill up your soul, but you have more than likely created a void in your life commonly referred to as breakfast, lunch and dinner. Some animal rights converts just decide to forge new food traditions. Certainly there is plenty of food variety available to explore, but what about those pancakes, that chocolate pudding and that bowl of Count Chocula®? Are they gone forever? We do not think so. Dairy substitutes are available and just like way back before you can remember when you had to adjust to cow's milk, so it is true that the dairy substitutes require adjustments in taste.

Mocha Mix® — Steve Allen likes it on his cereal; Jayne Meadows in her coffee. We cannot vouch for how healthy it is for you, but it contains no animal products.

A completely different route is using soy milk. Most health food stores and co-ops carry it in either dry or bottled form. Like all milk substitutes, it does not try to match milk vitamin for vitamin, but in and of itself, soymilk is a healthy drink and it can be used whenever milk is called for in cooking and even in drinking, though some of us have to reprogram our taste buds. Page 161 of the Basics chapter explains how to make your own soy milk. It is very easy to do.

If you're thinking of switching to goat milk to avoid contributing to animal oppression, you should know that while goats don't, at present, suffer from rigid confinement, the female is perpetually pregnant to maintain high levels of milk output. Her babies are taken from her when only a few days old, and many of the males are sold for slaughter (and currently served in some of Seattle's "finer" restaurants). The goat farm operation is usually smaller and not as high-tech as the dairy cow industry, but you couldn't exactly call this humanely produced milk, either.

Considering the facts that we have just presented about the dairy industry, it's ironic that a lot of us grew up hearing that a cow will not give milk unless she is happy. If the happiness factor was ever true in our past, breeders and scientists must have decided long ago to breed out such an unprofitable dependency. Washington's local agriculture officials have enthusiastically noted that Western Washington's dairy cows do not have to be happy any more to give us milk. One official went on to say dairy

---

I'm truly sorry man's dominion has broken nature's social union.

— *Robert Burns*

---

cows are in a long-term, high-stress environment, that it would not make any sense for cows' milk production to be correlated to stress since the modern conditions are so stressful.

But maybe the old tale about contented cows used to be true, and maybe science should take credit for making high production not dependent on happiness. Perhaps we have succeeded in upending nature's wisdom, which allowed us to receive a gift from a cow, only so long as the cow is well treated and happy. Perhaps the milk of human kindness has momentarily spoiled.

BUT THE GOOD NEWS IS YOU'LL HAVE 43%
FEWER INJURIES BEFORE YOU'RE SLAUGHTERED.

Eggs Benedict Arnold —
Cracking the Myth About Eggs

Bad news. Most eggs in Seattle (at least 90%, and probably more), come from "battery" hens on the modern farm. City dwellers know little about the egg business. The following description of the modern farm illustrates how far our concept is from reality.

Battery hens come four or five stuffed in an enclosed 12" by 18" cage (about 1/3 square foot per bird). The chicks that are to fill these cages hatch at a hatching factory. Then they are promptly sold to another factory — that belonging to the egg farmer. Once there, they are debeaked; that is, their upper beaks are sliced off with a hot iron. This is done to prevent cannibalism in the crowded cages. Properly done, it is painful. If done poorly, it results in blisters in the mouth, painful soft-tissue growths and burned tongues, all of which inhibit the bird's ability to eat or drink and can end in malnutrition and starvation. Some farms will also use the hot blade to cut off toes at the first joint; again to counter the aggression due to the crowded cages. Having four or five hens in a small cage is rather like watching a bubbling pot. There is constant competition to be on top where it is cooler and easier to breathe. Over time, with each bird successively popping to the top, and then being pulled down by another pushing upward, they lose a good portion of their feathers from all the rubbing against the wire cage. The weakest bird in the cage never gets off the bottom and often her feet will grow literally locked around the cage's mesh floor — or she can suffocate under the other birds as she loses in the struggle to be on top. After approximately 1½ years of this life, tired and so overstressed and depleted from production that their bones can actually collapse, the hens are slaughtered for food. (Note: a free-running hen, by comparison, lives 10 to 15 years.)

The 90% figure, we believe, is a generously underestimated percentage for local eggs. The Seattle supermarkets buy their eggs from local egg wholesalers. The wholesalers we contacted get 100% of their eggs from battery-hen houses. The Washington State Agriculture Department knew of no sources of eggs from free-running, undebeaked chickens in this area. Furthermore, one wholesaler official questioned the need for free-running hens when the battery cage system works so well.

It may "work well," but of all the animal-raising practices factory farming has wrought, the system used for laying hens is perhaps the most completely cruel in its exploitation. Unfortunately, eggs are one food many animal-respecting vegetarians have traditionally seen as safe. A food where animals would not be harmed. Our notion is based on that image of happy barnyard animals running and scratching for food, and though the image was never completely true, it's never been further from the truth than it is today.

What caused things to change? Prior to World War II, it was discovered that adding Vitamins A and D to chickens' diets meant they no longer needed sunlight and exercise for growth and bone development. Large flocks of indoor birds were now possible. Demand for eggs and chickens was high during the war years, so the coops got even more crowded. The solutions to overcrowding came from feed and chemical companies. The newly-introduced cages were raised off the floor for easier manure removal. Debeaking machines were created. More productive laying hens were developed. As each idea caught on, larger and larger flocks (and profits) were possible, and more people turned to the battery system to where now it is seen as the norm in America.

Has (humankind) the right to reduce life to a bare existence that is scarcely life at all? Has he the further right to terminate these wretched lives by means that are wantonly cruel? My own answer is an unqualified no.

— Rachel Carson

Obviously, there are certain tough choices an ethical vegetarian must make about eggs. On top of all the cruelty and physical and mental deprivation of the battery houses, there are also problems associated with hatcheries. Whether you buy battery or free-running chicken eggs, the death of the male chicks must be conceded.

The problem starts this way:

In order to have laying hens, it follows that some eggs must be allowed to hatch. Once the chicks' sexes are determined, the males are "culled" —literally thrown right into garbage sacks and left to suffocate and die. (Tragically, in at least one case, a very large local hatchery sells their dead male chicks to mink ranches — another industry as you might have already guessed we do not subscribe to — where they are eaten by animals who will soon be skinned to become "fashionable" coats). It is only the rare pedigreed male chick that grows up to fertilize eggs.

And what of the female chicks? At the very least, 90% of these specially-bred egg-layers are fated to be battery hens. The remaining hens may or may not live decent lives. Some are still debeaked and overcrowded and made to overtax their capacity to lay eggs in hatcheries or on some organic egg farms. Even if they are not — even if they live outdoors, scratch for food and do other all-American chicken things, most of them will be soup or pet food inside of a couple of years.

In light of all these conditions, the first difficult choice you must make is whether you want to buy eggs at all. If you're inclined to give them up altogether, there is solace in all of the good-tasting foods still available to you. For your baking, there's an egg substitute called "Ener-G" egg replacer available in some grocery stores and most health-food stores and

Vegetarianism is not just a personal choice! As a feminist I am taking action against a system which is oppressive.

— Carol Adams

co-ops. (A note of caution: other egg substitutes like "Egg Beaters" contain albumin — egg whites. Read the label and avoid products with eggs sneaked into them.) Also, many recipes containing eggs can be made eggless. We have tried to include many of these in our cooking section. If you like creating without recipes, there are guidelines for cooking and baking covered in Baking Tips, p. 173. Cookbooks devoted to cooking without eggs are available in bookstores and libraries. It may not seem possible to live without eggs, but remember, most of the world does this every day, and animal-rights people everywhere are doing it by choice and with ease.

In spite of the egg substitutes and the possibility of living happily without eggs, you may still want them in your diet. We of the Animal Rights Action Committee also wrestle with such decisions and have had to choose where and when to make changes. Having free-running chicken eggs is a choice many of you and many of us may opt for, and if you do, take credit for considering an animal's well-being over your own convenience; for at the extreme of convenience come eggs from battery hens — one of factory farming's most thorough tortures of feeling beings, and from the perspective of suffering, as disagreeable as any meat-eating practice.

The other difficulty the animal-rights vegetarian has is knowing *where* to buy eggs, if you have decided you want them. Ironically, trying to find non-battery eggs in Seattle may be enough to convince you to give them up. It's not going to be an easy hunt, but there are sources and there are ways. You say you have seen ads for free-running chicken eggs in stores? Not surprising, but unless you or someone you trust has actually seen the hens, do not believe this. We have spent the past year running down promising leads. A lot of stores are continuing to sell these eggs, despite finding out their source is from battery hens; or farm hens that are not caged, but they are debeaked; or some other combination of unacceptable circumstances that keep the hens from being humanely raised. Sometimes you will see a carton proclaiming the eggs are from organically-raised chickens . . . Don't be misled. These are probably battery hens fed a gourmet diet. Unless you have evidence stronger than the vendor's word (often the vendor is deceived about the eggs, too), it is wise to assume the eggs come from a limiting environment. This may seem disheartening, but keep in mind that asking for humanely-treated, free-running chicken eggs is going to create a market, even in the big stores. And maybe in a year or two, this situation will be looking up considerably, as it is beginning to in other places. In the meantime, here are some tips for getting through today.

• To find your own source, try putting up an ad in the rural co-ops and feed stores. We know of some successes using this approach.

- Another rural tip. if you are out in the country, drive around and look for signs saying "fresh eggs." There are many families with surplus eggs from the family coop. Chances are they'll let you look around, too. Also ask your co-workers who drive in from the country to bring you eggs from sources near them.

- Shopping for fertile eggs may yield some positive results for you but you will probably end up compromising your principles. The major frustration is that many fertile eggs come from hatcheries, and most hatcheries debeak chickens. Most hatcheries also are not nice places for male chicks. So we can hardly endorse hatcheries.

In the past we have tried to make distinction between animals which we acknowledge have some value and others wich, having none, can be liquidated when and as we wish. This standard must be abandoned. Everything that lives has value simply as a living thing, as one manifestation of the mystery that is life.

— Albert Schweitzer

If you do learn of a source, ask if you can visit. That may not seem important, but we know of one case where a local, big-name egg supplier did not have the facilities for the free-running hens it or its retailers claimed. Or sometimes the hens are "free-running" but debeaked and crowded by the thousands into small areas. Another game is for a farmer to have 100 uncaged hens and 50,000 battery hens and then supply many more retailers with "free-running" eggs than 100 hens are capable of producing — so it pays to visit. Here's a handy list of questions to ask when you get there.

1. How many chickens do you have?

2. How many square feet of roaming space do the hens have? (It is nice to have one square foot or more per bird.)

3. Are the chickens debeaked?

4. Can the chickens scratch in the dirt? (This is something they instinctively do, but are denied doing in a battery system.)

5. How many eggs does a hen lay in an average week? (Any more than four is depleting and overstressing the hen — it probably means chemicals in the diet, too).

6. Are the eggs fertile? (A good sign the hens are not caged.)

7. Do you raise chicks yourself? (Young hens are usually purchased from oppressive commercial-hatching operations.)

8. Are there *any* caged birds on the premises?

9. Do the hens get natural light?

These are reasonable questions to ask in order to move away from the gigantic scale of exploitation existing on factory farms. However, eating eggs, any style, will never be exploitation-free.

Locally, no one can satisfactorily answer all nine questions, but those places that come close should be given support for sincerely trying. Beyond these questions, there are others relating to fertilizers, medicines and pesticides. These are technical and more related to *our* health, and not as much to Animal Rights. Many co-ops, however, may be able to tell you what to ask about and look for if you want to know this side of the issue, too.

Some people will tell you not to visit their farm — that you will be creating a health risk. If this is the case, tell the owner you will visit the farm, but you will not go inside the buildings. If the answer is still no, then you have reason to be skeptical. The Animal Rights Action Committee of the Progressive Animal Welfare Society would be grateful for information on any egg seller you have doubts about or that you wish to commend.

Obviously, if more people are asking for these eggs, sources will develop over time, and finding them will not be difficult. One other possibility, should you have the space and time, is keeping your own chickens. They are not an overwhelming investment. You might even consider selling eggs. Without a doubt, there is a strong demand and surprisingly, a license to sell to retailers is inexpensive and the state agriculture department will show you how to weigh and size the eggs.

While it is true that ultimately, the decisions are yours, the animal rights perspective you should use to balance your decisions can be summed up in three words: quality of life. And what you decide in your personal life does make a difference.

Many of the facts and descriptions relating to battery hens in this section were drawn from the excellent book *Animal Factories* by Jim Mason and Peter Singer, © 1980.

Hidden Slaughterhouse and Dairy Products in Food

When you decide to become a vegetarian, the choices sound pretty simple, right? No meat. But there are likely to be animal products in refrigerator biscuits, refried beans, yogurt, and endless other foods. And sometimes the ingredient labels yield little information about the presence of animal contents.

For example, cheese is a natural choice to make if you decide to avoid meat dishes. But all cheeses contain a coagulant to make them firm — either animal rennet which is an enzyme extracted from calves' stomachs at the slaughterhouse, or a vegetable coagulant which is obtained from fungi cultures by fermentation. Animal rennet is most commonly used in aged cheeses such as parmesan, feta, romano, and most other foreign cheeses. Cheddar, mozzarella, and jack cheeses are usually coagulated with the vegetable version. The words to look for that will indicate a vegetable coagulant are "vegetable enzymes" or "rennetless." If you see the word "rennet," you can usually assume it is from an animal source. More specific examples are given in the list following this article.

You might not think that fruit-flavored gelatin desserts contain animal products, but gelatin is in fact derived from beef bones. There is a vegetable version of fruit-flavored gelatin available at health food stores that is more nutritious because it uses real fruit and contains no artificial preservatives or animal products. To substitute for unflavored gelatin, use agar-agar, also available at health food stores. Another product that contains animal gelatin is commercial yogurt — it usually gets its firmness from gelatin. A totally unexpected place to find gelatin is in Lucky Charms cereal; another is marshmallows.

Lard is used in refrigerator biscuits, many brands of refried and baked beans, most flour tortillas, and some shortening. Tallow, another form of beef fat, is found in Jiffy mixes. Anchovies are found in Worcestershire sauce, and Worcestershire sauce is found in many bottled salad dressings and sauces.

Gelatin and lard are generally easy to spot by reading labels, but there are several other terms which can describe a product either animal or vegetable in origin. Mono- and diglycerides can be made of vegetable or soy oil, or derived from animal fat. The label often won't specify which. These are found as thickeners in pudding and other mixes, frosting, frozen foods, ice cream, margarine, and some bakery goods. Other terms to be alert for are glycerine, lecithin, and natural flavoring. Several letters to food companies reveal that mono- and diglycerides, lecithin and natural flavorings are usually from vegetable sources.

If you are avoiding dairy products, watch for whey, caseinate, calcium propionate, and stearoyl, which are dairy by-products often used in margarine, "non-dairy" creamers or toppings, crackers, and baked goods. Lactic acid is a term for an acid originally discovered as a milk by-product, but currently it is usually synthesized from vegetable sources, so generally it shouldn't be of concern. Many "light" margarines are vegan, and eggless mayonnaise is available at most health food stores.

On some food packages, the word "Parve" will be visible near the product name. This Jewish term means the food contains no meat or dairy products, and is usually a good indicator there will be no hidden animal ingredients. Please note that "Parve" foods by definition *may* include fish and eggs, but rarely do, based on our visits to supermarkets in the Seattle area. A little more confusing is the use of the "Kosher" designation on some foods indicated by a "K" on the package. Theoretically, a Kosher

---

It's worthwhile (to note) that the major use of these chemicals in ham and sausage is to make them look nice and red — instead of the brown-gray they really are. Like putting lipstick on a corpse?

— from Everything You've Always Wanted to Know About Nutrition by David Reuben, M.D.

---

food containing dairy products will be marked K_D, and one which contains meat will be marked K_M. But "non-dairy" powdered creamers are commonly marked "K," even though they contain sodium caseinate and whey. And "non-dairy" sour cream substitutes are marked "K," but the Kosher gelatin they contain does come from beef. Consider a packaged food marked "Parve" to be free of hidden meat and dairy ingredients, but investigate further when you see a "K."

Some companies are consistent about using vegetable products; others will use whatever is most convenient at the time and will list all the different possible ingredients. Often, the surest way to find out what a product contains is to write to the company which manufacturers it. Staying away from highly processed foods will give you a better idea of what ingredients you are actually getting. Buying dried beans and grains, and fresh vegetables (or if they are frozen vegetables, stay away from ones with sauces) is usually a good method of avoiding hidden animal ingredients.

The following list was developed by extensive visits to Seattle-area supermarkets, and letters to food companies. Occasionally, a company will change its recipe for a product, so it's a good idea to check the ingredients of even those "safe" foods from time to time.

Item	Contains Meat or Meat By-Products	Vegetarian	Vegan
"Bacon"		Morningstar Farms Breakfast Strips (frozen) Worthington Stripples (frozen)	
"Bacon" Bits			Crescent Johnny's Lawry's
Baking Mixes	Most baking mixes contain lard or animal shortening	Bisquick Whole Wheat Roman Meal Harvest Recipe Multi-Grain Whole Wheat	
Beans (Refried & Baked)	Most contain lard, pork or bacon		Ashley's Refried Beans B&M Vegetarian Baked Beans Health Valley Chili Heinz Vegetarian Beans Hunts Chili Beans Rosarita Refried Beans S&W Baked Beans Chili Beans Maple Sugar Beans
Bean Dip	Most contain lard		Blue Bell Jalapeno-Flavored Hollywood Hain Jalapeno Bean Dip Hot Bean Dip Onion Bean Dip Granny Goose Amigos
Bouillon	Most is made from beef or chicken stock		Hauser Broth Instant Swiss-Formula Bouillon McKay's: Beef-Style Instant Broth and Seasoning Chicken-Style Instant Broth and Seasoning Romanoff MBT: Onion Bouillon Vegetable Bouillon Vegex Veg. Bouillon G. Washington's: Rich Brown Seasoning and Broth Golden Seasoning and Broth
Bread	Wonder: Country Style Regular (May contain beef fat or lard)	Most breads contain whey, sodium caseinate, butter or eggs.	Country Hearth: Bran 'n Honey Thin-Sliced 100% Wheat Francisco Extra-Sourdough Gai's: Honey-Wheat Olympic-Ridge

21

Item	Contains Meat or Meat By-Products	Vegetarian	Vegan
Bread (cont.)			Mrs. Wright's Grain Belt: Dill Rye 7-Grain Oroweat: Dill Rye Honey Wheat-Berry Old Country Deli Wheat The Little Bread Co.
		Middle East Pocket Bread	Most Pocket Bread
Bread Crumbs	Old London (animal shortening)	Devonsheer Italian Style	
Burgers (See "Fabulous Frozen Fakes")			
Burger Mixes			Fantastic Foods: Nature's Burger Tofu Burger Worthington Granburger (when reconstituted with water, resembles browned ground beef)
Catsup			Del Monte Heinz Kraft (The Natural Flavors contain no animal products)
Cereal	General Mills: Pac-Man Lucky Charms (Marshmallows contain gelatin)	General Mills Cinnamon Toast Crunch Kellogg Pop Tarts	Most cereals contain no animal products
Cheese	Brie Camembert Feta Fontina Havarti Jarlsberg Parmesan Provolone Romano Aged Swiss and aby Swiss (The above cheeses contain rennet) Kraft Cheez Whiz (Worcestershire Sauce) Ricotta (contain gelatin)	Brick Cache Valley Ricotta (contains no gelatin; available in bulk at some co-ops) Cheddar Colby Cream Cheese Edam Gouda Kuminost Monterrey Jack Mozzarella Washed Curd	Soyarella (non-dairy mozzarella) Neshaminy Valley Natural Foods, 421 Pike Rd., Huntington Valley, PA 19006 (or try your co-op)
Chili			Health Valley (canned) Fantastic Foods (in dry form)

Item	Contains Meat or Meat By-Products	Vegetarian	Vegan
Chips (Snack, Taco and Tortilla)	Cheetos (contains Romano) Doritos Nacho Cheese Tortilla (contains Romano and Parmesan)		Diane's Tortilla Hains Tortilla Health Valley Tortilla General Mills Bugles Corn Snack Mission Tortilla R.W. Knudsen Tortilla
Chocolate Chips		Baker's Semi-Sweet Chocolate Flavored Flickettes Chocolate Flavored Heath Bits 'O' Brickle Hershey's Milk Chocolate Semi-Sweet Chocolate Reese's Peanut Butter	Guittard Semi-Sweet Chocolate Lady Lee Semi-Sweet Chocolate Nestles: Peanut Butter Morsels Semi-Sweet Chocolate Morsels Town House Semi-Sweet Chocolate
Cookies	FFV Duplex Sandwiches (animal shortening) Keebler Grasshoppers (beef fat) Mother's Iced Molasses and Iced Oatmeal (gelatin) Nabisco Fig Newtons (may contain animal shortening) Peek Frean (beef fat) Sunshine Tru-Blue Cookie Sandwich Lemon (may contain lard) Vanilla (may contain lard)	Busy Baker Animal Crackers Archway Walnut Chocolate Chip Fred Meyer Whole Wheat and Honey Fig Bars Whole Wheat and Apricot Fig Bars Keebler Pecan Sandies Mother's Fig Bars Nabisco Chips and More Lorna Doone Pepperidge Farms Sunshine Butter Flavor Vanilla Wafers Hydrox Yum Yums	Archway Soft Molasses Archway Nutty Fudge Bunmaster Oatmeal Duncan Hines Almond Fudge Chocolate Chip Janet Lee Animal Crackers Sugar Wafers Scotch Buy Devil's Food Creme Vanilla Creme
Crackers	Busy Baker Honey Graham Keebler Honey Graham Most Keebler Crackers contain animal shortening Nabisco Chicken in a Basket Honey Maid Graham Premium Saltine (contains animal shortening) Ritz (contains animal shortening)	Ak-Mak Sesame Nabisco Cheese Nips Potato 'n Sesame Pepperidge Farms Goldfish Sunshine Cheese-It Krispy Saltine	Borden Melba Toast Old London Round Busy Baker FFV Stoned Wheat Wafer Janet Lee Saltine Keebler Wheatbury Wheat Snacks Manischewitz Dietetic Matzo-Thins Midel 100% Whole-Wheat Honey Grahams Nabisco Better Cheddars Onion Rounds Rye Rounds Wheatsworth

Item	Contains Meat or Meat By-Products	Vegetarian	Vegan
Crackers (cont.)			Norwegian Ideal Flat Bread
			Sunshine Honey Graham
			Ry/Krisp
			Sunshine American Heritage Old New York Style Rye American Heritage Old New York Style Sesame Honey Graham
			Triscuits
			Wasa Crisp Bread
			Wheat Thins
Desserts	Hostess Chocolate-Filled Cupcakes Fruit Pies Snoballs Twinkies (may contain animal shortening) Langendorf Fruit Pies (gelatin and lard) Mickey Mini Donuts (beef tallow, lard)	Archway Bunsmaster Cinnamon Rolls (98% egg-free) Morningstar Farms Mother's Pepperidge Farm Cakes Fruit Squares Pastries Turnovers Sunshine Most Van deKamp's Products	Mrs. Wright's Fruit Pies Western Family Fruit Pies
Eggroll Wrappers			Quon Yick Noodle Co.
Eggrolls (Frozen)			Health Valley
Fabulous Canned Fakes (see Meat Substitute section)			
Fabulous Frozen Fakes		Morningstar Farms Breakfast Links Breakfast Strips Grillers Totino's Nacho-Party Pizza Worthington Bolono Chik Stiks Dixie Dogs Fri Pats Leanies Meatless Salami Prosage Links and Patties Stakelets Stripples Super-Links Vegetarian Fillets Wham	Natural Touch Tofu Garden Patties New Leaf Tofu Burger Lifestream Vegi-Patties Pacific Soyfoods Soysage Worthington Chiketts (a sausage substitute) Mudpie Vegie Burgers
Falafel			Fantastic Foods Fred Meyer Bulk Mix Near East Sahara

Item	Contains Meat or Meat By-Products	Vegetarian	Vegan
Fillo Dough			All brands appear to be vegan
Frankfurters		Loma Linda Sizzle Franks Worthington (canned)	Loma Linda Big Franks (canned) Tofu Pups (frozen)
Frosting	Duncan Hines Canned Frostings	Lady Lee Frosting Mix	Pillsbury Artificial Vanilla Coconut-Pecan
Frozen Desserts	Mrs. Smith's Fruit Pies (contains lard)	Rich's Chocolate Eclairs Most Sara Lee Products Weight Watcher's Frozen Pies	Pepperidge Farm assorted fruit turnovers and fruit squares
Frozen Dinners	Some "Health One" frozen dinners (made by SeaTac Food Service)	Most "Health One" Frozen Dinners Health Valley Enchiladas Spinach Lasagne Stuffed Peppers Natural Touch Lentil-Rice Loaf Pepperidge Farms Vegetables in Pastry Broccoli with Cheese Cauliflower with Cheese Mushrooms Dijon	Birdseye Oriental-Style Rice
Frozen Vegetables	Bel-Air Broccoli Cuts with Cheese Sauce (contains Romano and Parmesan cheese) Cauliflower with Cheese Sauce (contains Romano and Parmesan cheese) Potato Wedges (animal shortening) Birdseye San-Francisco Recipe (chicken fat) Green Giant Broccoli in Cheese-Flavored Sauce (Parmesan cheese)	Bel-Air French Fries Potato O'Brien Tater Treats Ore Ida Crispers Golden Patties Potatoes O'Brien	Vegetables without sauces are vegan
Gelatin Desserts	Most are made from beef bones	Jello Chocolate Mousse Pie Olivier International Foods a la Mousse Chocolate	Hain Gel Dessert Salada Gel Dessert
Gravy			Crescent Brown Gravy Mix Mushroom Gravy Mix Kitchen Bouquet Browning & Seasoning Sauce La Choy Brown Gravy Sauce
Ice "Cream"			Ice Dream Albertsons Natural Strawberry Bar (Popsicle-type)

Item	Contains Meat or Meat By-Products	Vegetarian	Vegan
Ice "Cream" (cont.)			Island Spring frozen dessert Mocha Mix frozen dessert Rice Dream Yodolo (served "to go" only) Tofutti
Margarine		Most margarine	Cold 'n Soft Light Spread Hain Safflower Margarine Natural Food Store Soft Margarine Soybean Soft Margarine Nucoa Parkay's Light Spread Penny Smart Scotch Buy Light Spread (Safeway) Shedd's Spread Shop Rite Soya Lecithin Spread Table Maid Willow Run Soy Margarine
Marshmallow	most marshmallows contain gelatin	Kraft Marshmallow Creme Party Pride Marshmallow Creme	Seventh Day Adventist stores carry a vegan marshmallow: Emes brand
Mixes	Betty Crocker Black Forest Cake Chocolate-Flavored Eclairs All Stir 'n Frost Mixes contain animal shortening All Super-Moist Cake Mixes contain beef fat Jiffy (contains tallow) Pillsbury (beef fat) Mrs. Wright's (contains animal shortening)	Betty Crocker Big Batch Cookie Mix Chocolate Chip Golden Pound Cake (add eggs) Duncan Hines All Type Cakes (add eggs) Brownie Mix (add eggs) Cookie Mix (add eggs) Jello Instant Puddings (add milk) Puddings (add milk)	Betty Crocker Bake-A-Bar Krusteaz Scone & Shortcake Mix Pillsbury Poppin' Fresh Yeast Bread Mix Country White Golden Wheat
Non-Dairy Creamers & Sour Cream Substitutes	IMO (contains Kosher gelatin) Chivo (contains Kosher gelatin)	Most powdered creamers are vegetarian (contain sodium caseinate)	Mocha Mix (liquid) Rich's Coffee Rich (liquid)
Pasta		Golden Grain Stir 'n Serve Lasagna Dinner Kraft Macaroni & Cheese Lady Lee Macaroni & Cheese Lipton Butter Noodles and Sauce Cheese Noodles and Sauce Sour Cream and Sauce	DeLaurentiis (all varieties) Merlino's Mission (most pastas are vegan unless they have "egg" in the title) Westbrae Natural Whole Wheat Ribbons

Item	Contains Meat or Meat By-Products	Vegetarian	Vegan
Pasta (cont.)		Mission Fettuccine Macaroni and Cheese Noodle Roni Herb and Butter Romanoff Westbrae Natural Egg Noodles	
Pasta Sauce	Prego Italian Sausage and Fresh Green Pepper Chunks Plus Veal and Fresh- Sliced Mushrooms Ragu Chunky Gardenstyle Old World Spaghetti Sauce Westbrae Natural Tomato Sauce for Pasta		Johnsons Pasta and Pizza and Spaghetti Sauce Mission Spaghetti Sauce Prego Spaghetti Sauce Ragu Homestyle Spaghetti Sauce
Pita Bread		Middle East	Most brands are vegan
Rice		MJB Fried Rice Herb and Butter Rice A Roni Fried Rice Herb and Butter	Near East Rice Pilaf Rice A Roni Spanish Rice Uncle Ben's Long Grain and Wild Rice
Rolls		Gai's Butterflake Croissants Mrs. Wright's Sesame Sandwich Enriched Rolls	Gai's Freezer Rolls New York Bagel Boys Onion Pumpernickel Mrs. Wright's Honey Wheat Berry Rolls
Salad Dressing	Bernstein's 100% Natural Italian Restaurant Recipe Italisn (contain worcestershire sauce) Hidden Valley Ranch (mono- and diglycerides may be animal in origin) Kraft Bacon and Tomato Creamy Bacon Golden Caesar	Bernstein's 100% Natural Italian with Bleu Cheese Green Goddess Hain Buttermilk Caesar Natural Thousand Island Old-Fashioned Dressing Old-Fashioned Herb Kraft Creamy Cucumber Creamy Italian Lighthouse Creamy Italian Most Mayonnaise Nalley Thousand Island	Good Seasons Mixes Hain Honey and Lemon Italian Natural French Kraft Catalina French French Oil-Free Italian Zesty Italian (reduced calories) Lighthouse French Nalley's Red-Wine Wishbone French Italian Russian
"Salami"		Worthington (frozen)	
Sauce	Kraft Sweet and Sour Town House Barbeque Hickory Smoke Flavor Barbeque (all contain worcestershire sauce)		A-1 Steak (for your veggie burgers) Del Monte Chili Kraft La Choy Sweet & Sour The Jug Barbecue Pickapeppa

Item	Contains Meat or Meat By-Products	Vegetarian	Vegan

Sauce Mixes	Crescent Spaghetti Sauce	Knorr
		  Bearnaise
		  Swiss Hollandaise
		Lawrys Spaghetti Sauce
		Schilling
		  Spaghetti Sauce
		  Taco
			Crescent Taco
			Schilling
			  Chili
			  Meatloaf
			  Sloppy Joe

"Sausage"		Morningstar Farms (frozen) Worthington (frozen)	Pacific Soyfoods Soysage (refrigerated or frozen)
Seasoning	Cavender's All Purpose Greek Seasoning Johnny's Salad Elegance (Parmesan, Romano)		Johnny's Light Seasoning Salt Lawry's Pinch of Herbs Maggi Seasoning Morton Nature's Seasons Mrs. Dash Spike Vege-Sal
Shortening	Piedmont		Crisco Fluffo

Soups, "Vegetable"	Campbell's
	  Chunky Mediterranean Veg. (Parmesan)
	  Homestyle Vegetable (Beef Stock)
	  Manhandler Minestrone (Beef Broth)
	  Old Fashioned Veg. (Beef Stock)
	Knorr (in dry form)
	  Green Pea Soupmix
	  Leek Soupmix
	  Minestrone Soupmix
	  Onion Soupmix
	  (contain beef fat)
	Town House
	  Minestrone (Italian Veg.) (Chicken Broth)
		Campbell's
		  Cream of Asparagus
		  Cream of Celery
		  Cream of Mushroom
		  Cream of Potato
		Hain
		  Cream of Onion
		  Split Pea
		Hugli
		  Asparagus Soup Mix
		  Cream of Mushroom
		Mayacamas
		  Cream of Tomato
		  Cream Soup Base
		Progresso Minestrone (macaroni contains eggs)
		Town House
		  Cream of Celery
		  Cream of Mushroom
		  Cream of Potato
			Campbell's
			  Chunky Vegetable
			  Tomato
			  Vegetarian Vegetable
			Mrs. Grass Onion*
			Hain Cream of Mushroom*
			Health Valley
			  Bean
			  Minestrone
			  Vegetable
			Hugli French Onion*
			Knorr Vegetable Soupmix*
			Liption Onion*
			Mayacamas Green Pean*
			Natural Instant Miso Soup*
			  Natural Flavor with Seaweed
			Progresso Lentil
			Town House
			  Chunky Vegetable
			  Chunky Vegetarian Veg.
			  Tomato
			Westbrae Natural*
			  Brown Rice Ramen
			  Buckwheat Ramen
			*in dry form

Item	Contains Meat or Meat By-Products	Vegetarian	Vegan
Stuffing		MJB Stuffing Plus Herb and Butter with Wild Rice Stove Top San Francisco Style Rice-a-Roni Herb, Butter & Rice	Betty Crocker Traditional Herb Stuffing Kellog's Herb Seasoned Croutettes
Tortillas	Most flour tortillas contain lard	Western Family Flour	Most corn tortillas are vegan La Fiesta 100% Whole-Wheat Reser's Flour El Toro Flour
Whipped Topping		Cool Whip Janet Lee Whipped Topping Whipped Cream	
Wonton Wrappers			Quon Yick Noodle Co.
Worcestershire Sauce	French's Lea & Perrin's (both contain anchovies)		
Yogurt	Most house brands contain gelatin Lucerne lowfat yogurt (gelatin) Yoplait Custard-Style (gelatin)	Altadena Brown Cow Continental Dannon Lucerne Gourmet Mountain High Nancy's Yoplait (except custard-style)	

The best philosophical traditions in our culture say we should feel **something** in the face of violence and cruelty — guilt, remorse, compassion, shock, or outrage. But we are also encouraged to suppress those feelings when violence and cruelty supply us with meat. That twinge in the stomach remains, however, and it is not always easily suppressed. "It is a faint intimation," wrote Thoreau about his growing discomfort with fishing, "yet so are the first streaks of morning."

— The Vegetarian Alternative

Product Testing on Animals

The great majority of products that we use for cleaning and sprucing up both ourselves and our homes — from soap, deodorant, shampoo, toothpaste and make-up to floor cleaner, detergent and fabric softener —are tested on animals in a series of procedures which result in certain discomfort, prolonged suffering and frequent death for millions of animals annually in the United States alone.

Two routinely used procedures are the LD-50 and the Draize Test. In the LD-50 (which is short for "lethal dose in 50 percent"), groups of animals are force-fed with enough of the ingredient or product being tested to cause half of them to die within a specified time period, often two weeks. When the material being tested is relatively non-toxic, such enormous quantities are required to produce the desired mortality that it is not uncommon for animals to die from internal rupture caused by huge volume of material forced into them rather than from any acute toxicity inherent in the substance. Because an accurate "oral toxicity" level is the goal of this procedure, the test is usually repeated with several groups of animals — sometimes hundreds — for each substance tested. Even when an animal is clearly in agony and near death he/she is not humanely killed, but instead is allowed to linger in pain because anything else would invalidate the test results.

While all types of mammals, from guinea pigs to dogs, are used in the LD-50, rabbits are the standard animals used in the Draize "Eye Irritancy" test. Groups of rabbits are immobilized in stock-like devices, sometimes with their eyes held permanently open with metal clips for the duration of the test — commonly several days. The material being tested, often in concentrated form, is placed in one eye; the other eye is left untreated to act as a control. At the conclusion of the test period, the results — the visible ulceration or disfigurement of the eye — are rated.

Other frequently-used tests involve abrading animals' skins and applying a substance to determine skin irritancy; and an inhalation test in which animals are placed in chambers and forced to breathe mists of the test materials.

Virtually every major health-and-beauty firm routinely tests its newly-developed products and ingredients on animals before marketing to determine the LD-50, to categorize eye- and skin-irritancy, and so on. *But no law dictates that animal tests be used* for items such as cosmetics and their ingredients. These tests have been developed and promoted by the health-and-beauty industry itself — ostensibly to protect the public — but not incidentally to protect from lawsuits the companies which market these products.

The discovery of the law of evolution which revealed that all organic creatures are of one family, shifted the center of altruism from humanity to the whole conscious world collectively. Therefore, the practice of vivisection has been left, by that discovery, without any logical argument in its favor.

— Thomas Hardy

Alternatives to Supporting Animal Testing

It is practically impossible to find products which are completely consistent with the term "cruelty-free" simply because even if one company chooses not to test its products on animals, it is likely that the ingredients used have been tested by some industry- or government-sponsored lab at some time. Many ingredients which have been safely used for decades have only recently been tested on animals in response to industry's increasing reliance on laboratory tests.

In general, the consumer can minimize her/his support of animal testing by following these guidelines: (1) Select products with "natural" ingredients when possible. Although this does not guarantee that animal testing has not occurred, it does minimize the possibility, since highly synthesized ingredients are more likely to be heavily tested. (2) Buy from companies which rely on ingredients that have been used safely for many years, avoiding newly-introduced chemicals. (3) Support companies which state in writing that they do not test their products on animals, nor do they have any outside lab do so. Although such a statement is not a guarantee, it is probably the only practical method of learning which firms avoid animal testing. When corresponding with companies, ask specific questions and read the responses carefully — public relations people are usually adept at using the language. Recently, the manufacturer of a make-up line sold in many health-food stores has been issuing literature stating that it does not use animals for tests. While this particular company may not be using animals now, as recently as three years ago (presumably when the line was being developed and its "safety" needed to be established), this same company stated in writing that it did use animal tests.

Those companies which do develop products without using animals and which satisfy the Food and Drug Administration regulation that "each ingredient used in a cosmetic product and each finished cosmetic product shall be adequately substantiated for safety...," tend to be small family-run businesses which market a limited line of high-quality products. Because they lack the large chemical lab facilities available to the larger firms, they are generally incapable of synthesizing new chemicals for use in their products. Instead, they rely on ingredients that have been used for years and fall into the "GRAS" (generally recognized as safe) category. In addition they commonly use natural ingredients: natural flower essences for fragrance, natural colors, and in some cases, little or no chemical preservatives whenever possible.

Only a couple of companies offer home cleaning products that have not been tested on animals. Theoretically, at least, the consumer can discourage the development of new cleaning agents, and thus the testing of new substances on animals, by choosing "old reliables" such as ammonia in preference to "new-and-improved" cleaners.

We should remember in our dealings with animals that they are a sacred trust to us from our heavenly father. They are dumb and cannot speak for themselves.

— Harriet Beecher Stowe

Animal-Derived Ingredients

Product testing isn't the only way in which the health-and-beauty industry uses animals. Recently, a big selling point for many of the major cosmetics firms has been the inclusion of animal proteins in shampoos, conditioners and skin lotions. These and other cosmetics frequently contain many hidden animal-derived ingredients.

Apart from the dubious aesthetics of applying dead animal extracts to the body for beautifying purposes, there are several other good reasons for avoiding such ingredients. These extracts are generally obtained from the carcasses of slaughtered animals. The purchase of products with animal derivatives supports both the raising of animals for slaughter and the slaughter of wild animals — in other words, money talks. Even on other levels, the merits of applying animal proteins to the hair or skin are at best debatable. Protein molecules are indeed the building blocks of the body, but it is extremely unlikely that when applied externally they can be incorporated into skin or hair. So in addition to everything else, the purchase of products with animal-derived ingredients is often simply a poor beauty bargain. With some ingredients, there may be a health factor as well. Animal fat, or tallow, is routinely used as a base for products such as soap. Toxic residues from herbicides, pesticides or other chemicals accumulate and are concentrated in the bodies, especially the fat, of animals exposed to them. So using such products may increase a person's exposure to certain toxic materials.

Some other companies intentionally avoid animal-derived ingredients for ethical, economic or aesthetic reasons. Such companies offer products based on delightful arrays of herbal and nut extracts and oils. A few companies are now distributing lists of ingredients used along with an explanation of where and how each is derived. This is especially helpful since some ingredients (such as amino acids, stearates and glycerine) can be obtained from either animal or non-animal (i.e., plant or synthetic) sources; so without information from the manufacturer, it is impossible in many cases to know the origin of an ingredient listed on a label. "Natural" does not necessarily mean "cruelty-free." Mink oil, animal protein and animal tallow are all natural, yet all are obtained by raising and slaughtering animals; "natural" glycerine is usually animal-derived.

Common sense and perserverence are needed when attempting to locate cruelty-free companies. One firm recently wrote us that it uses no ingredients of animal origin, yet, "hydrolyzed animal protein" was prominent in the list of ingredients enclosed in the letter. The president of another company was honest enough to write that the keratin in his conditioner is supposedly obtained from human hair rather than from other animals, but he was "not so sure." A third manufacturer emphasized that his company uses no dead-animal-derived ingredients, while at the same time promoting bovine (cow) tissue and various glandular extracts featured in the company's products.

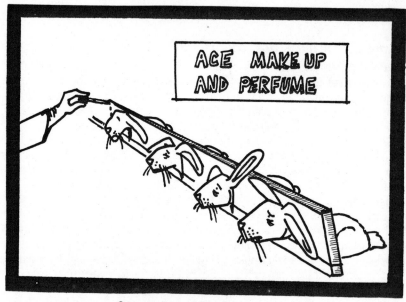

COSMETIC VALUE.

Particular attention should be directed to observations for the presence of tremors, convulsions, salivations, diarrhea, lethargy, sleep, coma, food consumption and body weight changes, especially if survival exceeds one day.

— Principles and Procedures for Evaluating the Toxicity of Household Substances in Reference to the LD-50 Test

A Local Source: Bodkins!

Seattle is very fortunate to have a local source of cosmetics and bath products that are guaranteed to be cruelty-free. Bodkins is an English firm with a branch located at 517 Olive Way, Seattle, 98101 and one in Gilman Village, Issaquah, 98027. Bodkins has produced a range of skin and hair care preparations from safe and easily understood ingredients, without artificial colors, animal ingredients, or animal testing. Their selection includes shampoos, fragrances, moisture lotions, soaps, bath oils, bubble bath, and hair styling gel. Call them at (206) 340-0127 for more information.

Origin of Cosmetic Ingredients

The following lists include only some of the more commonly used cosmetic ingredients. As a general rule, an ingredient which can be obtained from either animal or non-animal sources should be assumed to be from an animal source unless the label or correspondence from the manufacturer indicates otherwise, since the animal derivative is often cheaper.

Ingredients of Animal Origin

Animal Protein	Keratin
Ambergris	Lanolin*
Collagen	Mink Oil
Elastin	Musk
Hydrolyzed Animal Protein	Tallow
Isopropyl Lanolate*	

*Lanolin and its derivatives are obtained from sheep's wool.

Either Animal or Non-Animal Origin

Amino Acids	Nucleic Acids
Biotin	Oil
Cetyl Alcohol	Palmitic Acid
DNA	Panthenol
Enzymes	Polypeptides
Fatty Acids	Protein
Glycerine, Glyceryl Stearate	RNA
Guanine	Stearates
Lecithin	Stearic Acid
Mono- and Di-Glycerides	Urea
"Natural" Sources	

Non-Animal Origin

Aloe Vera	Shikakai
Carageenan	Synthetic Musk
Chalk	Soy Derivatives
Clay	(Soy Protein, Lecithin, etc.)
Comfrey	Vegetable Mono- and Di-Glycerides
Gum Benzoin	Vegetable and Nut Oils
Henna	Vegetable Protein
Horsetail	Witch Hazel
Jojoba Oil	Xanthan Gum
Paraffin	

... The sad part of most animal cruelty — it is perpetuated through history and tradition and very few of us stop to question it — and certainly the animals can't do anything about it ... Here's something else to think about — cruelty is not only painful to the animals, but it demeans those who inflict it and those who support it.

— from "Gleeb" in the Seattle Times,
August 28, 1982
by Paul Lowney, PAWS Member

Cruelty-Free Manufacturers

Although there is probably no manufacturer which is completely "cruelty-free," these companies have stated in writing to us that they do not test their products on animals, nor do they have any outside lab do so. In addition, they have stated that they use no ingredients of animal origin, with the exception of lanolin (from sheep's wool), and honey and beeswax derivatives in some products. Names of manufacturers which sent inconsistent or incomplete responses have been omitted from this list.

These products are available in Seattle-area stores, usually co-ops or health food stores, unless otherwise noted.

Company	Address	Phone Number
Autumn Harp	28 Rockydale Road, Bristol, VT 05443 .... (802) 453-4807 *Skin care, balm and salve, baby care.*	
Auromere	1291 Weber Street, Pomona, CA 91786 .... (714) 628-8255 *Chandrika soap, Vicco toothpaste.*	
Beauty Without Cruelty, Inc.	180 Pool St., Biddeford, ME 04005 .... (207) 282-6966 *Cosmetics, hair care, foam bath, lotions, cologne; mail order only. Cruelty-free statement on label*	
Biokosma	*Made in Switzerland, available in some stores locally. Skin and hair care, soap.*	
Bodkins, Ltd.	517 Olive Way, Seattle, WA 98101 .... (206) 340-0127 228-2nd Avenue S.W., Pacific, WA 98047 Gilman Village, Issaquah, WA 98027 .... (206) 392-8867 *Skin and hair care, cosmetics, bath and perfume oils.*	
Body Love	P.O. Box 2711, Petaluma, CA 94952 .... (707) 795-8174 *Skin care. Note: may contain yogurt; read the labels.*	
Community Soap Factory	Box 32057, Washington, D.C. 20009 .... (202) 387-6933 *Liquid soap, shampoo. Mail order only.*	
Country Comfort	2317 Bluebell Drive, Santa Rosa, CA 95401 ...... (707) 945-1970 *Baby care, balm, salve.*	
Dr. Bronner	P.O. Box 28, Escondido, CA 92025 .... (714) 745-7069 *Soaps*	
Golden Lotus	2800A S. Shoshone, Englewood, CO 80110 ...... (303) 761-0174 *Skin and hair care, home cleaners (laundry soap, all-purpose, dish soap, fabric softener).*	

The Herbalist	6500 20th N.E., Seattle, WA 98115 . . . . (206) 523-2600
	An herbal product store stocking Borlind of Germany, a cruelty-free line of cleansers, toners, creams, foundation, cover-stick, and sun care. Also carries Weleda — cruelty-free hair care, soap, creams, and baby products.
Kiss My Face	P.O. Box 804, New Paltz, NY 12561 . . . . (914) 246-5011
	Soap
Loanda	114 Hamilton Dr., Novato, CA 94947 . . . . (415) 883-1235
	Soap. Note: Milk 'n Honey Bar contains milk.
Martha Hill Cosmetics	c/o Trudy Beaman
	100 Pine St., Holmes, PA 19043 . . . . (215) 461-0282
	Skin care. Mail order only.
Montage	1514 Pike Place, #14 . . . . (206) 624-9446
	(across from the Pike Place Market)
	Carries Bare Essentials® brand of cruelty-free cosmetics. They also sell Montage® brand soaps, shampoos, conditioners and lotions that have not been tested on animals, but may contain animal protein, so check the label. Their perfumes are also cruelty-free.
Nature's Gate	9740 Cozycroft Ave., Chatsworth, CA 91311 . . . . . (213) 882-2951
	Skin and hair care, deodorant, toothpaste. Nature's Gate is widely available at health food stores and states on the label that it has not been tested on animals nor does it contain animal ingredients. Note: avoid products in their "Aloegen" line which may contain animal derivatives.
Rainbow	170 Wilbur Place, Bohemia, NY 11716 . . . . (516) 589-5563
	Hair care. Note: avoid their soaps, which contain animal tallow.
Shikai	P.O. Box 2866, Santa Rosa, CA 95405
	Shampoo. Note: Avoid the conditioner, which contains keratin of uncertain origin.
Sirena Tropical Soap	Box 31673, Dallas, TX 75231 . . . . (214) 243-1991
	Soap
Soapbox	University: 4340 Univ. Way NE
	Seattle, WA 98105 . . . . (206) 634-2379
	Downtown: Seattle Trust Court, 3rd & Marion
	Seattle, WA 98105 . . . . (206) 623-1795
	Pike Place Market: 1916 Pike Pl.
	Seattle, WA 98102 . . . . (206) 441-5680
	Many cruelty-free shampoos, lotions, soaps and cosmetics. Most store personnel are knowledgeable about brands that are exploitation-less.
Sombra C&S Laboratories	5600G McLeod, N.E., Albuquerque, NM 87109 . . . (505) 884-1417
	Make-up foundation and blush. Note: contains lecithin which may be derived in part from eggs.
Bonnie Steward	860 Valley View Pl. S.W., Issaquah, WA 98027 . . . (206) 392-9338
	Local distributor of Golden Lotus products; i.e., home cleaners (laundry soap, all-purpose, dish soap, fabric softener). Also Beauty Without Cruelty products, i.e. deodorant and fragrances. Other items available by special order. Call for an appointment.
Tom's	Railroad Ave., Kennebunk, ME 04043 . . . . (207) 985-2944
	Skin and hair care, mouthwash, toothpaste, deodorant, soap, shave cream. Note: Tom's did do some animal tests in the past, but has stated that they have no intentions of doing so in the future.

Velvet	P.O. Box 5459, Beverly Hills, CA 90210 .... (213) 472-6431 *Moisturizing/shaving lotion. Mail order only.*
Vita Wave	7131 Owensmouth Ave., Suite 94-D Canoga Park, CA 91303 .... (818) 886-3808 *Hair colorings, permanent wave solutions, conditioners.*
Weleda	841 S. Main St., Spring Valley, NY 10977 .... (914) 352-6145 *Skin and hair care, deodorant, toothpaste, cologne, soap, baby care.*
Windflower Herbals	P.O. Box 987, Columbia, CA 95310 .... (209) 533-2238 *Salve, balm, poison oak/ivy treatment.*
Zenith Supplies	6319 Roosevelt Way NE, Seattle, WA 98115 .... (206) 525-7997 *A variety of New Age health supplies, including exploitation-less creams, lotions and perfume oils.*

Much of the information contained in this list was obtained from the *Beauty Without Cruelty* Charity Newsletter, 175 W. 12th St., New York, NY 10011.

Pro-Animal Lifestyle

A philosopher once remarked that she found it a sobering thought that animals could do without people, yet people would find it almost impossible to do without animals.[1] Avoiding meat is just one aspect of vegetarian living. If you wear leather, fur, scrimshaw jewelry or a down jacket, have a lambskin seat-cover, or use a popular oven cleaner, you are using products that are obtained from dead animals, or tested on live ones.

Animal products are everywhere. One clear example of this is in footwear. If you go to a department store, your selection of leather shoes is endless — but if you are looking for cloth or synthetic ones, the supply is more limited. From down-to-earth shoes designed with comfort in mind to high-fashion footwear, leather has become the sign of quality. And even when not integral to the construction of the shoe, leather is often added as decorative trim.

For years we have purchased these shoes, yet what we don't think of when we buy them is that they come at the expense of other living creatures. Much of the leather in shoes comes from cow and pig carcasses at the slaughterhouse. The argument many people use that "the animal was killed for its meat, anyway" won't hold true in a discussion with a vegetarian. Then there are eels, lizards, snakes, alligators and crocodiles — not killed for meat, but killed solely so that a small part of each skin can be made into shoes (or a purse or wallet) to be worn as a status symbol by humans.

There are alternatives. A non-leather choice in footwear will most likely be nylon, canvas, rubber, urethane, vinyl, or a combination thereof. Careful shoppers can find athletic shoes which are comfortable, waterproof and leather-free. Nylon and rubber are good choices for their ability to repel water. Vinyl and urethane are attractive and do make a good dress shoe, but they are often at a disadvantage for their inability to bend and breathe well. Some department stores feature a pretty good selection of non-leather brands, which will be mentioned at the end of this chapter. Budget-type stores such as K-mart, Fred Meyer, etc., often have a wide

---

[1] Ruth Harrison, *Animals, Men and Morals: An Enquiry Into the Maltreatment of Non-Humans*, eds. Stanley and Roslind Godlovitch and John Harris (New York: Taplinger Publishing, 1972), p. 11.

selection of cloth and synthetic styles. A shoe must designate "All Materials Man Made" if it is not made of leather, so look for this label. Again, pay attention to comfort when trying on a shoe of synthetic materials, because it will not adapt to your foot the way leather will. Keep an eye out for hidden leather — often the upper part of a shoe will be fabric, but the soles will be leather. If you find a department or shoe store salesperson who is knowledgeable about comfortable non-leather shoes, you will have found a gold mine. And the advantage of explaining your interest in alternative footwear is that it lets store personnel know there is a market for such products.

As to other accessories, watch for belts, purses, briefcases, wallets, and gloves made of fabric or synthetics. They are sturdy and stylish.

Those who, by their purchases, require animals to be killed have no right to be shielded from this or any other aspect of the production of the meat they buy. If it is distasteful for humans to think about, what can it be like for the animals to experience it?

— Peter Singer

Furs

Furs have a glamorous and elegant reputation. But the truth is that the 35 to 65 pelts of mink needed to make one coat[2] did not magically transfer from the animal to the finished garment. Most fur in the U.S. comes from animals raised in captivity, or "ranch raised." Chinchilla, mink, rabbit and fox are bred in captivity where they are kept in small cages in crowded conditions. Although the least painful method of killing farmed furbearers is injection of sodium pentobarbital,[3] the lives of the vast majority come to an end by means such as crude homemade electrocution devices, a broken neck, injections of poison, and cyanide administered orally. Care is taken not to damage the pelt, but little thought is given to providing a quick and painless death to the animal unfortunate enough to be born with a coat humans find pretty. No laws protect ranch-raised furbearing animals such as these.

As bad as they are, our own country's indiscretions are certainly equalled by those on other continents. One of the oldest, cruelest forms of fur ranching is the raising of Persian lamb. The lambs must be killed within five days after birth to keep their fur tightly curled. These animals, also known as Karakul or Swakara, are not raised in the United States; however, many of their furs are imported. Broadtail, a product of Asia, is from naturally or artificially aborted lambs. Abortions are sometimes induced by beating a pregnant ewe.[4] Elsewhere, there have been recent attempts to ranch ocelots in captivity, even though they are an endangered species.

---

[2] Greta Nilsson and others *Facts About Furs* (Washington, D.C.: Animal Welfare Institute, 1980), p. 77.

[3] Cleveland Amory, *Man Kind? Our Incredible War on Wildlife* (New York: Harper and Row, 1974), p. 259.

[4] Amory, *Man Kind? Our Incredible War on Wildlife*, p. 262.

Though the largest percentage of furs comes from "ranched" animals, pelts are also taken from wild animals who have been trapped. Millions of coyote, mink, bobcat, raccoon, muskrat, beaver, rabbit and other wild animals are caught in the steel jaw leghold trap every year. While this trap has been banned in numerous countries, only a few states in the United States substantially limit its use. Washington is not one of these. State laws regulating how often traps must be checked (to see if they are sprung) vary from every 24 hours, to once a week, to not at all. These laws are nearly impossible to enforce. In many instances, the trapped animal is left for days in panic and pain. Some chew off their own leg in an attempt to escape. Not only does the trap spring on target animals, but it will also catch any bird, cat, dog, or other animal unfortunate enough to step into it. Up to 7 out of 10 animals caught in the steel jaws may be non-target animals, or "trash," as trappers call them.[5] Household pets are often victims; even if released, they usually die of blood poisoning. Those that do live are likely to have their limb amputated.

It may have been difficult reading these details, but they are essential in making an informed choice. Fur is a luxury, not a necessity, and most people would probably avoid fur garments if they knew more about the methods of the industry.

An issue the public hears much more about is the killing of seals. Seals are killed for their fur by Canada, the United States, the U.S.S.R., Japan, Uruguay, Chile, Norway, and South Africa[6]. The National Oceanic and Atmospheric Administration (N.O.A.A.) has jurisdiction over the North Pacific fur seal hunt by the Aleut Indians in the Pribilof Islands off Alaska. Seals are annually driven inland, clubbed, and skinned. Negotiations began in 1985 which may succeed in reducing this hunt to subsistence level for the Aleut natives. And largely due to public protest, this year's Canadian seal kill was reduced to 20,000 despite a quota of 186,000.

In other parts of the world, exotic animals, including cheetah and ocelot, are trapped and killed and their furs are exported to the United States.

[5]Nilsson, *Facts About Furs*, p. 90.
[6]Nilsson, *Facts About Furs*, p. 71.

Hidden Animal Exploitation

Nearly every food additive and household cleaning and freshening ingredient has undergone toxicity tests on live animals. Some examples are notable. Nutrasweet (aspartame), the newest low-calorie sweetener found in soft drinks such as Diet Coke, dessert mixes, low-calorie cereal, and hot cocoa mixes, has been tested extensively on laboratory animals. And the tests *aren't* limited to just food and cleaning ingredients. Even gasoline companies have announced that harmful gas fumes were tested on live animals.

The fact is, the newer the product, the more likely it is that animal testing has occured. This makes a good argument for sticking to basic cleaners and foods which have been on the market for a long time, and which do not contain coloring, preservatives or artificial sweeteners. In addition to this rule of thumb, there *are* several excellent detergents, shampoos, soaps and cosmetics offered by some local distributors, who take care that their products have neither been tested on live animals nor contain animal ingredients (with the possible exception of lanolin from sheep's wool, honey, or beeswax). Their addresses and product lines are listed on page 36 to 38 of the chapter titled Product Testing on Animals. More information on humane alternatives is listed at the end of this chapter.

It is not only in products run through testing laboratories where unsuspected animal exploitation exists. Abuses are hidden in other industries, like the wool industry for example. True, wool is not *always* obtained at the expense of a sheep's life, nor is the lanolin used in cosmetics and lotions — though both products are often taken from sheep carcasses at the slaughterhouse. But even when sheep are not killed for their wool, the modern shearing process is violent, cuts up the skin — and if shearing takes place during the wrong season, exposes the sheep to cold to which they cannot adapt. Another dark side of the wool/sheep industry that we support when we buy wool is the vicious and controversial response sheep ranchers have to the predators of sheep — namely the poisoning, trapping and shooting of coyotes. For these reasons, you might wish to consider wool substitutes. Cotton makes a wonderfully warm alternative to wool in sweaters. In general, it is easier to find cotton clothing in the late winter and spring, while wool garments are marketed heavily in the fall. Polypropylene clothing is a good wool substitute which is found at sport shops, and is excellent for its ability to resist absorbing moisture.

Also to be considered are the entertainments we support; circuses, rodeos and those movies which exploit animals. Wild animals are taken out of their natural environments, confined, subjected to the stress of travel and made to perform tricks for human enjoyment. Moviemakers often call for stunts which injure or kill animals (horses are made to fall using trip wires). The biggest problem is that they treat these animals without respect in the name of entertainment. Lions weren't meant to jump through a hoop.

Where do you draw the line in treating our fellow creatures humanely? It is not easy to know. Think of honey bees, who produce honey as a food for themselves. Some are injured or killed every time their hive is opened to obtain honey. Even this could be considered inhumane. And silk. Silk is made by silkworms to form their cocoons. As larvae, they are killed by steam or hot air to keep their cocoon intact. The resulting silk is beautiful, but it is obtained at the expense of the lives of those silkworms. Raw silk, on the other hand, is made from cocoons abandoned by the adult moths. Buying raw silk garments rather than refined silk is less exploitative and is one more step many people would choose to take toward more harmless living.

"FIRST HE SAYS HE'S DOING THIS FOR US, THEN HE SAYS TO SHUT UP AND GET FAT."

Hidden Animal Ingredients

Vitamins can be a source of added nutrition, but they are usually composed partially of animal by-products. Vitamins A and D are commonly derived from fish-liver oil, while several of the B vitamins are the products of beef liver. Calcium and other minerals and vitamins often come from bone meal, and there are a host of other animal parts, including bovine brain, adrenal gland, enzyme, kidney, heart and testes concentrate dried into tablet form for human consumption. For most of these animal-derived vitamins, there is an alternative vegetable source. A and D, for example, can be derived from carrot-root powder. Another source of A is palm oil. Most of the B vitamins are available from whole rice and brewers yeast, and C is safe — it is always from a plant source (rose hips or corn, usually). Enzyme preparations can be obtained from papaya, and calcium and other minerals can be synthesized from inorganic salts, or sometimes derived from autolyzed yeast. The key is to read the label; pick a brand of vitamin that lists the ingredients — not all of them do. And remember this — just because a vitamin is advertised as vegetarian does not necessarily mean that it is free of animal products. Sometimes these will contain fish-liver oil. And other times, you may find vitamins which state that they would be a good supplement for a vegetarian's health, but the tablet itself contains animal ingredients. Another thing to watch for is capsules enclosing vitamins — they are usually made of gelatin, which is obtained from beef bones. There are companies which are careful to avoid animal derivatives, and several suppliers are very specific about which products are totally animal-free. Their names follow this chapter.

Other hidden animal ingredients are not intentionally hidden; rather, people have not stopped to think about where the product comes from. For instance, goose down in comforters, sleeping bags and jackets really does come from geese that have been slaughtered. Synthetic substitutes have been developed which are less expensive, have more loft than down and resist water better. Brand names are Hollofil® and Quallofil®. Polyfill pillows are humane alternatives to those stuffed with feathers. Most new vegetarians will probably not abandon the leather shoes, feather pillows and other animal products they have accumulated over the years. But when the time comes to replace them, a non-animal choice can be made.

Consider the source of the jewelry we wear. Pearls are taken from oysters; scrimshaw jewelry is carved on whale teeth and walrus tusks. The tusks of elephants are used in ivory jewelry and other decorations. Animals have been killed for centuries for their ivory, but with imitation ivory now available, arguments for using animal ivory are unfounded. Another humane alternative may be to buy jewelry made from antlers of animals who shed them regularly, thus no pain or loss of life is involved. Some elk antler jewelry is so obtained. But before buying any antler product, be certain that it is not a product of cruel exploitation.

The listing of hidden ingredients also includes marine oil from fish, whale or porpoise fat, which is often used as a lubricant and as an oil base in paint. Blood from slaughtered animals is used as an adhesive in plywood, foam rubber and pharmaceuticals. Catalase, an enzyme from cows' liver, is an ingredient in some food wrappers. Elmer's Glue has a cow on the label — the glue is made from the casein in milk. Many brushes used for hair, shaving, cosmetics and paint are made of animal hair. Fish and bone meal are used as fertilizer. Catgut from sheep intestines is used in surgery as absorbable suture material. Carpet padding is commonly made of horse hair; gelatin is used in making camera film. Most sports equipment, such as balls and gloves, is made of leather. It is almost impossible to live totally free of products made from animals.

Many other unexpected uses of slaughterhouse by-products are detailed in an article entitled "Hidden Animal Products," by Andis Robeznieks, in *Vegetarian Times*, Nov. 1985. The article is reprinted in *The Animals' Agenda*, Dec. 1985.

The weight of this information is overwhelming and too much for anyone to absorb all at once. Our point in presenting it is not to overwhelm, but to inform. Knowledge is power. Aren't we better off knowing the full relationship animals play in our lives? The more we discover about the ways animals are used and abused, the more humane choices we can make. If we let our feelings be known about our concern for animals, eventually more products will be made animal-free. Every step taken toward more humane living enlightens us and integrates us into our world.

How can ethics become the basis for a world philosophy? When it relates to the entire world . . . the basic concept on which goodness rests is reverence for all life . . .

— *Albert Schweitzer*

Some information for this article was taken from "Animal Ingredients and their Alternatives"; Nermin Buyukmihci, Barto, PA. The author can currently be reached through People for Ethical Treatment of Animals, PO Box 42516, Washington, DC 20015.

Credit is also due to the "Non-Animal Product Report," Marcia Pearson, Seattle 1977. Marcia can be reached at Fashion with Compassion, Box 268, Bothell, WA 98041.

DRESSED TO KILL.

Catalog	Product	Address
Amberwood	Cruelty-free cleaners, cosmetics vitamins, belts, wallets, books	(404) 461-8576 125 Shoal Creek Road Fayetteville, GA 30214
Beauty Without Cruelty Newsletter	Quarterly update on cruelty-free living	175 W. 12th Street Suite 16G New York, NY 10011
Cotton Dreams	Cotton clothing for infants, children, adults	Box 1261-AA Sebastian, FL 32958
Deva	Miscellaneous cotton clothing	Box F83 M Burkittsville, MD 21718
Esprit	Women's clothing, shoes and boots	950 Tennessee Street San Francisco, CA 94107
Haband	Men's dress shoes	265 North Street Paterson, NJ 07530
John Blair Menswear	Men's dress shoes	Warren, PA 16366
Johnny Appleseed	Women's shoes and gloves	50 Dodge Street Beverly, MA 01915
Jollys	Cork clogs	Emi Meade 16000 Fern Way Guerneville, CA 95446
J.R. Carlson Laboratories	Vitamins (catalog specifies which are vegetarian)	Dept. V1 15 College Drive Arlington Hts., IL 60004
My Brother's Keeper, Inc.	Skin and hair care, cosmetics, vitamins, baby, household and pet products	(317) 962-5079 P.O. Box 1769 Richmond, IN 47375
The Natural Formula Book for Home and Yard	A book containing recipes for household cleaners using natural ingredients	Rodale Press Emmaus, PA 19049
Nevada Nutritional	All-vegetarian vitamins, minerals, protein and fiber supplements	(702) 331-5595 1533 Greg Street Sparks, NV 89431 —or— (415) 778-2983 200 J Street Antioch, CA 94509
Plus Products	Mostly vegetarian vitamins, including an A-D-E combo	(213) 991-8303 Malibu Junction Store 29002 Old Agoura Road Malibu Junction, CA 91301
Red Cross Shoes	Women's dress shoes	(212) 244-9501 Hushpuppies c/o Wolverine World Wide 350 Fifth Avenue New York, NY 10018
Sandak	Women's cork sandals	(714) 734-6400 1195 Pomona Road Corona, CA 91720

Schiff	Large line of vitamins, many are vegetarian; also found in most health-food stores	(201) 933-2282 121 Moonachie Avenue Moonachie, NY 07074
Solgar	Vegetarian vitamins	(516) 599-2442 410 Ocean Avenue Lynbrook, NY 11563
Vanguard BSC Footwear	Men's dress shoes	Sunningdale Sound Leicester LE3 1UR England

Local Sources

	Shoes
Chubby & Tubby	Various athletic shoes
Hardy Shoes	Several synthetic men's styles
House of Woks and Bowls	This Pike Place Market shop has a myriad of oriental-style men's and women's non-leather shoes
K-Mart	Men's, women's, and children's styles
Kinney's	Men's, women's, and children's styles
Lamont's	Red Cross® dress shoes are synthetic.
M.J. Feet	The "sporty" Birkenstock sandal is the only style that is leather-free. May have to be special-ordered.
J.C. Penney	Men's, women's, and children's styles
Volume Shoe Source	Large percentage of synthetic shoes
	Vitamins

The following companies supply health food stores and Fred Meyer Nutrition Centers (most of their products are vegetarian). Included are addresses in case labels do not specify ingredients.

KAL	Canoga Park, CA 91304
Natures' Plus	10 Daniel Street, Farmingdale, NY 11735
Plus Products	2681 Kelvin, Irvine, CA 92714
Schiff Products	Moonachie, NJ 07074
William T. Thompson	Carson, CA 90745
	Household Cleaners & Personal Hygiene
Bodkins, Ltd.	Cosmetics, skin and hair care, bath and perfume oils. All products are cruelty-free. An excellent local source.
Fred Meyer Nutrition Center	Sells a few soaps, shampoos, deodorants and toothpastes that are cruelty-free. Check "cruelty-free manufacturers' list" for brand names.
Mari-Don Healthway	Sells a few soaps, shampoos, deodorants and toothpastes that are cruelty-free.
Phinney St. Co-op	Sells laundry detergent, dish soap, all-purpose cleaners and shampoo.
Soap Box	Sells a few soaps, shampoos, deodorants and toothpastes that are cruelty-free
Bonnie Steward	Sells soaps, laundry detergent, dish soap, all-purpose cleaner, and fabric softener. Her home number is 392-9338; work 643-8887.

Co-ops and Health Food Stores

Where do you buy the alternative products we have described in other sections of this book — the foods, household and beauty items that haven't been created at the expense of animal life or animal suffering? Though some supermarket chains are now stocking animal-free products, often your best choices will be found in health-food outlets and food cooperatives. In Seattle, you will find a plethora of health-food stores to choose from, as well as a few co-ops. In these stores, you can usually buy many of the product lines we recommend. But we warn you — come informed about the brands you want, especially in reference to health-and-beauty aids as, with only one exception we know of, stores do not separate cruelty-free items from those having been tested on animals —and this type of information you won't find printed on the label. Please also remember that the designation "health food," or "natural ingredients" does not necessarily mean cruelty-free. See our chapters titled "Product Testing on Animals," and "Vegetarian Living" for more detailed explanations of humane purchasing, and for lists of cruelty-free product lines. Finally, with product in hand, never forget to read the label for possible slaughterhouse ingredients, even checking products you thought were safe.

The obligations of law and equity reach only to mankind; but kindness and beneficence should be extended to the creatures of every species, and these will flow from the breast of a free man, as streams that issue from the living fountain . . .

— Plutarch

Most health food stores carry a limited and often expensive selection. Convenience (quick-fix) foods, vitamins, packaged grains and snacks, as well as "natural" health-and-beauty aids are the main items; but many also carry some bulk foods and refrigerated goods. Co-ops are member-owned stores that can usually buy many items in bulk and pass on savings to customers. Nonmembers are almost always welcome, though they are not entitled to the same discount as are members. Membership, however, is usually an easy process, normally requiring either a small participation fee or a few volunteer hours. Co-ops vary in their diversity, but most carry many foods in bulk that you can normally find packaged in a conventional store. Such foods as grains, beans, nuts, oils, pastas, honey, spices, cheeses, etc. are regular fare. You can also buy dairy, produce, local breads, health-and-beauty aids, as well as some packaged items at most co-ops.

"WHAT DO YOU WANT TO DO TODAY HENRIETTA ?"

In general, health-food stores and co-ops, even though they cater to a large number of vegetarians among their clientele, do not purchase and sell based on a "humane" policy, but rather on standards of health alone. If they have free-running eggs to sell you (though we hasten to say that they are not, in this this area, likely to have a genuine source of free-running eggs — see the chapter titled "Eggs Benedict Arnold — Cracking the Myth About Eggs") it is the merit of the healthier egg they promote, not the chicken's standard of living. Usually no signs separate cruelty-free products from others. Therefore, we suggest you express your concerns. Let store personnel and management know why you buy vegetarian, and perhaps help educate them by providing them with the names of products that meet your standards and ask that they designate shelves for cruelty-free items. By doing this, you will also be helping suppliers who have a concern for animals by pointing out the added advantage of cruelty-free products.

Since not many stores are outstanding in their concern for animals, we will not attempt to review every health-food store in Seattle, but we'll clue you in to a few. If there is a store in your own neighborhood you feel deserves special mention (e.g., carries no meat or designates "humane" products), please let us know so that it can be included in a future edition.

> *If someone decides to become a vegetarian because they fear that meat is poisoning their body, then the results of their decision are beneficial . . . If, however, a person becomes a vegetarian because of a concern for the welfare and life of a domestic animal, then I feel I could place more trust in their judgment and consideration for the care of all living things.*
>
> — David Hancocks

Cooperatives

Phinney Street Co-op
400 N. 43rd, Seattle, Washington *633-2354*

This is the only store in Seattle we know of that is all vegetarian and has a humane policy. Phinney Street Co-op is non-profit and volunteer run. Besides making a conscious effort to purchase cruelty-free, ecological and political guidelines are also adhered to when buying from suppliers. Local and organic product, bulk grains, legumes, flours, spices and cheeses (most rennetless), and more, are usually available at good buys. You will be amazed at the savings on spices. All food products are vegetarian, and Phinney Street Co-op only carries health-and-beauty aids that are cruelty-free. The co-op isn't perfect, but the effort is there and the policy is definitely progressive.

Central Co-op
1835 12th, Seattle, Washington *329-1545*

In the past, Central did not sell meat products. Now a few items are carried, though the policy is controversial among membership, so we may be looking at a change back to a "meatless" policy in the near future. Foods are very reasonably priced, especially spices, and even though there is not a humane policy, expect more sensitivity to animal issues here than at most other stores. Bulk flours, pastas, beans, nuts, etc. Cruelty-free health-and-beauty aid lines are not separated from other lines. So again, be familiar with humane brand names.

Puget Consumers Co-op (PCC)
Greenlake: 6518 Fremont N., Seattle, Washington *789-7144*
Kirkland: 10718 N.E. 68th, Kirkland, Washington *828-4621*
Ravenna: 6504 20th Ave. N.E., Seattle, Washington *525-1450*
Seward Park: 5041 Wilson Ave. S., Seattle, Washington *723-2720*

PCC co-ops do carry meat products. Compared to other city co-ops, PCC stores are fairly large with a wide selection of packaged and bulk "health foods" as well as dry goods. Some cruelty-free health-and-beauty aid lines are available as well as others that are not cruelty-free. As in most stores, they are not separated from each other and there is nothing designating which products are cruelty-free and which aren't.

Health-Food Stores

There are health-food stores all over Seattle, all offering food a
vegetarian can eat. Few stick out as having a real humane policy, though
we're sure that as more stores become aware of the distinctions between
cruelty-free items and items that are not so humanely produced, we'll be
seeing a change in what many health-food stores carry. Generally, store
personnel have shown interest when we have approached them on the
topic.

Your yellow pages will give you ample selection of health-food stores, so
choose one to suit your needs which is convenient to you; but we would
like to mention the following stores as being notable and suggest you look
them over if you're ever nearby. We find that a store that offers a variety in
bulk items with which we can expand and explore our vegetarian menus,
as well as offering a particularly large supply of vegetarian packaged foods,
is an especially good resource for the vegetarian shopper.

Fred Meyer Nutrition Center

Fred Meyer has a special "nutrition center" in several of its Seattle-area
stores. Items carried usually include a selection of packaged food, along
with a variety of bulk items, including beans, grains, flours, pastas, etc.
Especially pleasing to some vegetarians are the textured vegetable
proteins carried in dry bulk. Substitute "bacon bits," "beef granules," and
"ham chunks" are available at a fairly low cost. Usually, the stores have a
frozen section in which items such as fruit pies, vegan "TV dinners,"
pizzas, etc. can be found. Among health-and-beauty aids, there are no
signs separating cruelty-free products from others, though some cruelty-
free lines are carried.

Garden Grocer

4217 University Way N.E., Seattle, Washington *634-3430*

This is a fairly large and comprehensive market with many vegetarian
and vegan items. A good selection of bulk foods, ranging from legumes
and nuts, grains, flours, pastas, to nigari (a coagulant for making tofu).
Packaged products are also carried, along with local brands. As well as
having a refrigerated section, there are also "deli" items including
packaged salads and sandwiches to eat on the go. Many cruelty-free
health-and-beauty aid lines are sold, but they are not separated from other
lines that exploit animals — so customers must know what to shop for.

International District

We suggest a walk through some of the shops in the International District. You will find several foods that are new to you, including produce, that you can adapt to vegetarian recipes, and of course, many ethnic foods that are traditionally vegetarian. Canned meat substitutes made out of gluten (most others we have referred to are made from soy) are available in many stores.

Magnano Foods
1501 Pike Place Market (mezzanine) *223-9582*

Magnano's does not carry any meat. They do, however, carry a very good selection of pastas, whole grain flours, refrigerated items, spices and snacks.

Manna Mills
21705 66th West, Mountlake Terrace, Washington *775-3479*

A good place to shop for those living in south Snohomish County or north King County. Bulk grains, flours, beans, nuts, TVP, oils; also packaged varieties. Especially good prices on some bulk foods, and often a good place to pick up that hard-to-find item. Some cruelty-free health-and-beauty aids; again, not separated from others.

Mari-Don Healthway Natural Foods
1900 N. 45th Street, Seattle, Washington *632-7040*

Another favorite source of meat substitutes for vegetarians in the Wallingford/University districts. The store offers a large selection of canned and frozen vegetarian foods, including vegie hot dogs, burgers, and eggless mayonnaise. There are also vegetarian vitamins, as well as cruelty-free health-and-beauty aid lines, though there is no separation on shelves between cruelty-free and noncruelty-free brands.

Minglement
Vashon Island *463-9672*

Natural-food source on Vashon Island, carrying bulk and packaged foods, as well as several cruelty-free health-and-beauty aid lines mixed in with others that aren't cruelty-free. Carries bulk herbs and spices, herbal pet supplies, and vegetarian dog food.

Mother Nature's Natural Foods
516 1st N., Seattle, Washington *284-4422*

This Queen Anne store offers a good selection of vitamins, minerals and other health and beauty aids. (Check for cruelty-free brand names.) The lunch bar features vegetarian chili, soup, and sandwiches such as lentil loaf.

Northgate Health Foods
727 East Northgate Drive, Seattle, Washington *365-7590*

This store is located in the Northgate shopping mall, and carries a variety of products including packaged grains, spices, flours, pastas, etc., and a large selection of canned meat-substitute products by Worthington and Loma Linda. The store also has freezer and refrigerator sections and does have some cruelty-free health-and-beauty aid lines — they are not designated as such, neither are they separated from other lines.

Rainbow Grocery
409 15th East, Seattle, Washington *329-8440*

At the top of Capitol Hill, the Rainbow offers a good selection of reasonably-priced produce, bulk, and packaged goods. Very good buys on spices and produce. Cruelty-free health-and-beauty aid lines are also available — not separated from other lines.

Seventh Day Adventist ABC Book Stores
Bothell: 20015 Bothell Way S.E., Bothell, Washington *481-3131*
Auburn Academy (ask for Adventist Book Center):
  5000 Auburn Way S., Auburn, Washington *833-6707*
  (open only Tuesday and Thursday, 12:00-6:00 pm)

These stores are totally vegetarian, stocking a wide array of canned, packaged, and frozen meat substitutes. Foodwise, there isn't much else. The prices are low, and twice a year they have "stock-up sales." The major brands available at ABC are Loma Linda and Worthington, and many people we know will buy by the case — stocking up at great savings on, for instance, canned "vegie hot dogs" to last a year. Read the labels if you are vegan, as many items have dairy and egg ingredients, and read the chapter in the book on meat substitutes, p. 77, for more information about what to look for in "fake meat."

The Souk
Seattle: 1916 Pike Place, Seattle, Washington *623-1166*
U-District: 4142 Brooklyn Ave. N.E., Seattle, Washington *633-4400*
Lake City: 7825 Lake City Way N.E., Seattle, Washington ... *527-5332*

Middle-Eastern and Indian foods (located across the street from the Pike Place Market, and in Lake City). Exotic foods and ingredients for your middle-Eastern recipes. Bulk and packaged food.

Sunrise
5202 University Way N.E., Seattle, Washington *527-4141*

Carries a good variety of bulk grains, flours, beans, etc., and also packaged goods. Quite willing to supply special requests.

Produce Markets

You don't have to depend upon supermarket produce sections. Savings can go up along with the quality of selection if you find the right produce market, or small grocery store that specializes in produce. For example, try Rising Sun Farms Produce (6505 15th N.E.) and Rising Sun Too (1831 E. Madison). Also, Ballard Produce (6319 24th N.W.), S&M Market (2201 Queen Anne N.), and of course, the Pike Place Market.

Though, as stated, there is still a lack of knowledge among many store personnel concerning the extent to which animals may have been exploited by some of the companies represented on their shelves, we also feel that these store people, who specialize in offering alternative products to the community, can also be open and responsive to concerns we make known to them. It is up to us, then, to provide them with the information on testing and animal ingredients that the companies themselves don't advertise, and to let them know that we want those cruelty-free products available to use and that they be clearly designated on shelves marked "cruelty-free." Until there is public demand for humane products, we will probably not see a total switch over in most stores to all cruelty-free items. Most businesses will not take such a risk unless they are fairly sure there is a potential market for their wares. So if you want to be able someday to walk into a store without reading labels and searching your memory, remember to make your tastes known. When that day of worry-free shopping comes, it will be a nice day for you, but most important, it will be a much, much nicer day for animals.

"KIDS, OVER YONDER IS WHAT WE REFER TO AS INTELLIGENT LIFE."

"SHE EATS LIKE SUCH A <u>HUMAN</u>."

Restaurants

"Hold the meat, please!" The Seattle area has over 2,000 restaurants; most of them serve only entrees that used to walk around. But the vegetarian should not despair, there are many possibilities for a meal sans meat, fish or fowl. We offer suggestions to help in that pursuit.

1. **Plan ahead.** Call restaurants — ask if they serve vegetarian meals, have salad selections or a-la-carte items.

2. **Be imaginative.** Cafeterias give the selective diner an array of choices. Brunches are being offered by many restaurants (usually on weekends) and there are fruits, breads, salads and desserts to feast on. Occasionally, the casseroles will be meatless, but it is a good idea to ask before plate piling.

3. **Try ethnic.** Italian, Mexican, Middle-Eastern, Indian, Ethiopian, Chinese, Vietnamese or Thai or other Asian food usually has some vegetarian selections. Some places will substitute a meatless sauce if you ask.

4. **Be flexible.** Occasionally, you may be in a situation where you left your sprout sandwich and gorp bars at home, you have an animal-rights meeting to go to immediately after work, or whatever the reason, and you find yourself faced with the golden arches. (Maybe someday the sign will say, "40 billion soyburgers sold.") When the closest fast-food chain is your only choice, you can stick to the salad bar, potatoes and onion rings (but you might want to ask about the fried foods to see if they were cooked in lard — many are). If you like Mexican food, the best fast food bet in Seattle is Taco Time. Their larger outlets have a new, expanded menu with rice, enchiladas, bean entrees and most have an excellent selection of items. They will substitute beans for meat, and we are told no lard is used in the beans or in the fried products — in contrast to other Mexican restaurants. (And in time, Seattle's vegetarians may prevail upon them to use lardless flour tortillas — until then, stick to corn tortillas). Pizza places will make just about anything you want (Why does it seem they charge more for a vegie pizza?) and even leave off the cheese, if you insist.

5. **Be assertive.** Last, but not least, it is important to be a vegetarian advocate. That doesn't obligate you to scream out at posh restaurants, "But I don't eat baby calves, bunnies, turtle soup or fish eggs!" It does mean you ask for vegetarian meals because you don't want to eat meat, fish or fowl. Encourage the establishments that offer choices by thanking the employees, telling your friends and relatives about them, and patronizing them again and again. If you are shy, write on the bill, "Thanks for serving a vegetarian meal."

Man is the only animal that can remain on friendly terms with the victims he intends to eat until he eats them.

— *Samuel Butler*

Additional Tips:
Traveling and Vacations — Eating on the Road

1. Major airlines offer "special meals," which you ask for when buying your ticket. They usually ask if you want vegetarian or vegan. You take your chances with the food offered, but at least the airlines are trying.

2. Take food with you whenever possible. Opt for the motel room with the kitchenette, use what you brought or raid the local grocers. (On a recent trip some of us made through cattle country, we feasted on delicious vegie entrees — freeze-dried or dehydrated — purchased from a Seattle recreational co-op. We supplemented with fresh fruits and breads purchased on the road.)

3. Resorts and hotels are getting more fitness and health-oriented, and some offer vegetarian cuisine for their health-conscious guests. Hint: California is years ahead of Washington in this regard.

4. When traveling and you don't want to carry food, there are always a few vegan stand-bys in most grocery stores. (Ovo-lacto vegetarians always have cheese, canned ravioli and spaghetti, potato and macaroni salads, desserts and salads to select from.) Of course, fresh fruits and even some fresh vegetables come to mind. A jar of peanut butter goes nicely with the above, or more commonly, with bread or crackers. Chips and salsas are filling. Cold vegetarian beans or Progresso soups are a change of pace. Some canned vegetables, such as three-bean salad can be tasty. Dried raisins, fruits and nuts are great snacks and don't need refrigeration. When your will is weak, check some of the cookie labels — especially the cheap, generic brands — you may find a surprise vegan treat among them.

Another Tip:
Eating Out at Friends' and Relatives' Homes

Aunt Ruthie knows you're a vegetarian because you told her, but she just sat you down in front of some suspicious refried beans and marshmallow salad. Well, what are you going to do? Set Aunt Ruthie straight, knowing that would embarrass her, or swallow hard and dig in? We've all got our own styles, and you know your friends a little better than we do, but more than likely, Aunt Ruthie made beans and marshmallow salad instead of roast beef and shrimp salad — and she made them especially because you're a vegetarian.

Such a scene is probably in your future. And it is a tough one to figure out. You might want to consider rewarding Aunt Ruthie's good intentions. You don't want to make her think your lifestyle is hard or unpalatable. If you enjoy her meal, you've advanced vegetarianism, at least the concept of vegetarianism, in her mind — and that, after all, is our goal (and, we suspect, the farm animals' goal, too).

In the same vein, some of us vegans who are strict in our own homes are not strict about dairy products when we eat at someone else's house. It's a strategic choice. Our goal is to promote vegetarianism; to get our foot in the door and be able to talk about animal issues. We feel that a meat eater who invites us to dinner is making an effort in cooking vegetarian for us. Vegan cooking may seem too much of an obstacle for them. If it is, they may not ask us to dinner — and they may never attempt to cook vegetarian. We, in turn, will lose an opportunity for the topics of vegetarianism and veganism to come up. And most likely, they will never know how easy it is to cook a vegetarian meal. Our goal is to build a bridge, not to preach from an island. And you never know — by keeping a door open, you may also create a new channel of communication and awareness that someday may even address the politics of dairy cows and marshmallows, too.

. . . and then I found myself realizing, with an amazement which time has not diminished, that the "meat" which I was accustomed to regarding like bread or fruit, or vegetables — as a mere commodity of the table, was in truth dead flesh — the actual flesh and blood of oxen, sheep, swine, and other animals that were slaughtered in vast numbers

*— from Seventy Years Among the Natives
by Henry S. Salt, whose writings
compelled Gandhi to promote
vegetarianism as moral reform*

A Glossary of Ethnic Vegetarian Foods

An unexpected benefit to vegetarianism is discovering great food traditions which aren't all-American. We're especially fortunate in large cities like Seattle where specialty restaurants can thrive. Over time, one realizes certain ethnic restaurants are expected to feature certain traditional vegetarian foods. To give you a head start on knowing what you can generally find in these establishments, we've compiled a list of some of the more common ethnic vegetarian foods available in Seattle.

Chinese

We all know about fried rice, chop suey and chow mein which can be made vegetarian upon request at most Chinese restaurants (that is, if they aren't already vegetarian), but don't forget these commonly available vegetarian items.

Egg Foo Yung — Bean sprouts and onions in egg batter, fried like a patty and served with sauce (ask about meat in the sauce).

Humbow — (Often made with vegetables.) Chopped, spiced vegetables wrapped in a steamed bun (ask about lard in the bun).

Indian

Alu Mattar — Spiced and sauced potato chunks and peas.

Chapati — Pancake-shaped, unleavened whole-wheat bread cooked over a flame.

Chole — Garbanzo beans often served in tomato sauce.

Dal — Lentil or yellow split pea soup. Several variations.

Pakora — Spiced vegetables mixed with bean flour and deep-fried.

Panir — Mild Indian cheese. Found in many main dishes.

Pappadam — Very thin lentil flour tortillas which are deep-fried. Served with appetizers.

Paratha — Folded pancake-like wheat-flour bread which is cooked over a flame. Sometimes stuffed with spiced vegetables.

Pulau — Delicately spiced rice, often made with almonds and raisins.

Puri — Pancake-shaped wheat-flour bread. Deep-fried until it puffs up.

Rayta — Sliced cucumbers in yogurt and spices.

You have just dined, and however scrupulously the slaughterhouse is concealed in the distance of miles, there is complicity.

— *Ralph Waldo Emerson*

Mexican

If you find a place which doesn't use lard in its beans or tortillas, then of course, tacos, burritos, guacamole and nachos are always available. But be on the lookout for these often-vegetarian foods, too:

Chile Rellenos — A mild green pepper filled with cheese or eggs, dipped in batter and deep-fried.

Sopapillas — Flour dough, deep-fried until it puffs out. Served with honey and butter (watch out for lard in the dough).

Tostada — Pretty much like a taco, but with a flat tortilla. Sometimes guacamole replaces beans.

Ethiopian

Injera — A flat, very light bread.

Wat — Means stew, and it can be made to go with any vegetable.

Middle Eastern

A few years ago, Middle Eastern food was as foreign to Seattle as . . . well, the Middle East; but now these restaurants abound, especially in the University District.

Baba Ganooj — A dip made of pureed, baked eggplant, garlic and sesame butter. Eaten with pita bread.

Dolmathes — Stuffed grape leaves.

Falafil — Ground up beans and spices, shaped into spoon-sized balls, deep-fried and served with a spicy sauce and vegetables.

Hummus — A dip made of pureed garbanzo beans and sesame seed butter. Eaten with pita bread or fresh vegetables.

Labneh — Yogurt and garlic.

Pita — Another name for pocket bread.

Tabouleh — Middle Eastern salad made of bulgur, parsley or mint leaves, tomato and garlic.

Thai

Hot and Sour Soup — The hot is pepper. The sour is lemongrass or vinegar. Add a little tofu and you've got a basic hot and sour.

Pad Thai — Thin rice noodles with eggs and vegetables with an indescribable peanut sauce.

Vietnamese

Cha Gio — Fried spring roll or eggroll stuffed with lettuce.

Japanese

Yakisoba — Fried noodles and vegetables. Not always vegetarian.

Italian

You probably grew up with pizza, spaghetti, ravioli and lasagne. But that's not all there is to know.

Calzone — Kind of an enclosed pizza. Calzone means "diaper." Get it?

Pesto — Sauce of basil leaves, garlic, olive oil and pine nuts or walnuts. (Watch out for parmesan cheese, which contains rennet.) Often served with pasta.

Eastern European

Pirogie — A stuffed dumpling. Also called Vareneki. Can be filled with vegetables or cheese.

Piroshki — Fried dough, which can be stuffed with cheese or vegetables.

Raising animals for food contributes most of this country's water pollution burden; production of meat requires 20 times as much water and eight times as much energy as the equivalent amount of vegetable protein.

— Veg. Information Service

Restaurants: A Dining Guide to Seattle

We wish this section was filled with meatless restaurants. Some places we've listed offer only one or two choices, but because there are so few restaurants that are 100% vegetarian, we've included many of these which also offer, as a rule, at least one and usually several vegan entrees. As we have mentioned, if it's salad or even eggs or cheese you're wanting, you can dine most anywhere. We are sorry if we left out anyone's favorite vegie hangout; let us know and we will include it next time. This guide is provided as a resource for the consumer. It is not meant to promote one restaurant over another. This is the last section of this book to be completed — to make it as up-to-date as possible. Nonetheless, it's always good to call ahead because the restaurant business changes every day.

Ali Baba's
West Capitol Hill: 707 E. Pine 325-2299
Open seven days a week. Sundays dinner only.

One of Seattle's good Middle-Eastern restaurants with great ethnic flavor. Never tried falafil, hummus, baba ganooj or stuffed grape leaves? Well, you'll just have to. Wonderful spicy food!

Alpine Health Foods
Mercer Island: 7611 S.E. 27th *232-7900*
Open weekdays for lunch

A lunch-only restaurant. Serves variety of soups, chowders and sandwiches, and with the exception of tuna, everything is vegetarian. Try the meatless taco salad and the "shamburger" sandwich.

Axum
U-District: 4142 Brooklyn N.E. *547-6848*
Open seven days a week. Sundays dinner only.

The variety of the big city allows for *two* Ethiopian restaurants. One is Axum, which serves several vegetarian meals including: the spinach-lentil plate; the yellow split pea plate; the collard green plate and the cabbage, carrot and tomato plate. The delicate injera bread is also available. Axum is located in the Brooklyn Square building.

The Bagel Express
Near Pioneer Square: 205 1st Avenue S. *682-7202*
Open seven days a week. Closed by 7 p.m.

Vegetarian soups. Hummus and avocado-cream cheese sandwiches and, of course, a variety of bagels.

Bahn Thai
Near Seattle Center: 409 Roy *283-0444*
Open seven days a week. Saturdays and Sundays dinner only.

Thai restaurant. Ethnic noodle, soup and rice dishes. Try the peanut sauce, hot and sour soup and ethnic desserts. Separate vegetarian menu. Friendly service.

Bangkok Hut I
Downtown: 170 S. Washington Street *624-7565*
Monday through Friday lunch and dinner.
Saturday dinner only. Closed Sunday.

Bangkok Hut II
Belltown: 2126 3rd Avenue *623-4425*
Monday through Friday lunch and dinner.
Saturday and Sunday dinner only.

There is so much Thai food available in Seattle. Both restaurants have several vegetarian selections, include a napa cabbage dish and "Bangkok Garden" (mixed vegetables).

The Boarding House
Kent: 211 S. 1st *854-0707*
Open Monday through Saturday for lunch. Friday for dinner.
Closed Sunday.

All we can say is Broccoli Pie.

Byblos
Downtown: 2311 5th Avenue *682-9745*
Open Monday through Friday for lunch and dinner.
Saturday dinner only. Closed Sunday.

Falafil, hummus, baba ganooj and dessert. Middle-Eastern food.

Cafe Counter Intelligence
Downtown, across from Pike Place Market:
94 Pike, Suite 32 (3rd floor above the Corner Market) *622-6979*
Open Monday through Saturday for late breakfast, lunch and dinner.

You're going to have to hunt to find this place, but once you do, order fruit and cheese plates, vegetarian soups, shirred eggs, dessert and espresso. Yes, we like their name, too.

Cafe Loc
Near Seattle Center: 407 Broad *682-7663*
Open Monday through Friday for lunch and dinner.
Saturday dinner only. Closed Sunday.

Has a separate vegetarian foods section on the menu. Lists 20 dishes. Reasonable prices. Tasty and attractive Vietnamese entrees. Great spring rolls. Friendly service. (Cafe Loc is also located in the Seattle Center "Center House." Open seven days a week.)

Cause Celebre
Capitol Hill: 524 15th Avenue E. *322-1888*
Open seven days a week for breakfast, lunch, and dinner.

The Cause Celebre is an informal place with tables outside and inside. You order at the counter. Its selection of food includes stir-fry, Middle-Eastern foods, calzone, sandwiches — also quiche and soup. In fact, the only things on the menu which are unvegetarian are tuna and salmon. Delicious desserts (homemade ice cream), sundaes, shakes and pastries. Many beverages, hot and cold. Sunday brunch is 8:00 a.m. until 2:00 p.m.

The Curry House
U-District: 4142 Brooklyn Avenue N.E. *633-4400*
Open Monday through Saturday for lunch and dinner. Closed Sunday.

As you might guess by the name, this is an Indian restaurant. Reasonably priced vegetable entrees, served with rice and papadam. Snack menu is entirely vegetarian with breads, samosas and dips. The Curry House is located in the Brooklyn Square building, and is adjacent to The Souk, an Indian, Middle-Eastern grocery store.

El Cafe
U-District: 6106 Roosevelt Way N.E. *526-2434*
Open seven days a week for breakfast, lunch, and dinner.

Mexican food. They will convert any recipe on request. Vegetable and/or cheese rellenos and vegetable and/or cheese enchiladas. They also make an interesting acorn squash with nuts, raisins and mushrooms (tell them to leave the chicken out of this and they will). El Cafe uses no lard in either their beans or their flour tortillas! Their vegetarian soups have a vegetable stock. Great!

Elliott Bay Cafe
Pioneer Square area: 101 S. Main (downstairs) 624-6600
Open seven days a week for lunch and dinner.
Breakfast Monday through Friday.

With a bookstore upstairs and shelves of browsing books and newspapers below, Elliott Bay is a great place to take your time over a meal. Hummus and a few sandwiches are available, plus salads and breads. Most days there's vegetarian soup.

Free Mars
Belltown: 2416 Western 441-1677
Open every day for lunch and dinner. Sunday brunch.

What you might call an informal restaurant. And surreal, graffittied and 50's-ish, if you will. The entire menu is vegetarian. Normally, there is a vegan entree (e.g. tofu tetrazini) and vegan soup. Also hummus and cheese-type sandwiches for lunch. Check into their desserts. Live music on Friday and Saturday nights. All the waitpeople are very unique and personable.

Geogy's Indian Cuisine
Lake City: 12345 Lake City Way 367-4694
Open Thursday through Monday for dinner.
Closed Tuesday and Wednesday.

Geogy's must use a phone booth for its quick changes. By day it poses as a standard American lunch-type place, but by night it transforms into an Indian restaurant with five traditional curried vegetable and other vegetable entrees on the menu. Now if it could only leap tall buildings in a single bound.

The Grand Illusion
U-District:

1405 N.E. 50th (inside the Grand Illusion Movie House) 525-9573
Open seven days a week for breakfast, lunch, and dinner.

Breakfast, soups, salads, breads and sandwiches.

Grand Palace
Downtown: 417 2nd Avenue 624-3825
Open seven days a week for lunch and dinner.

Thai restaurant. Curried vegetables and tofu. Noodles and vegetable soup.

Gravity Bar
Downtown:
86 Pine Street (across from Pike Place Market) 443-9694
Open seven days a week from 7 to 7

Juice bar. Tucked into a corner of the Pike Place Market. Just a wonderful selection of juices. Small menu with mostly vegetarian snacks (cheeses, breads and vegetables). And that's all. Wierdly and beautifully appointed.

Guido's Pizzeria
Green Lake: 7902 E. Green Lake Drive N. 522-5553

Fresh-baked, New York-style pizza. Get it by the slice or by the pie. They also serve meatless calzone. Salads available, too.

Hi-Spot Cafe
Madrona: 1410 34th Avenue 325-7905
Open for breakfast and lunch. Closed Tuesday.
Open for dinner in summer.

The Hi-Spot always has a vegie sandwich of the day. Sometimes they go all out and offer vegie soup, too. Many types of omelets are also available. Daily vegetarian entree. Most of the time they have vegie piroshki.

Honey Bear Bakery
Green Lake: 2106 N. 55th (55th & Meridian) 545-7296
Open Monday through Saturday 6 a.m. to 9 p.m.; Sunday 6 a.m. to 6 p.m.

Delicious bakery items, desserts, espresso, vegetarian soups and salads. Planning to expand the menu and keep it vegetarian! Live music on Saturdays.

India House
U-District: 4737 Roosevelt Way N.E. 632-5072
Open seven days a week for dinner.

If you've never eaten Indian food, welcome to the unexpected. India House is not inexpensive, but once in a while it's worth splurging for. Many vegetarian selections on the menu, including appetizers, dinners, soups, and very exotic breads and desserts. The mild food is mildly spicy. *The spicy food is spicy!*

International Society for Krishna Consciousness
Madrona: 3114 E. Pine 329-7011

Some of you might be interested in a free vegetarian meal. Every Sunday at 5:30 p.m. at the above address, exotic vegetable dishes and desserts are served.

Jerusalem Family Restaurant
Belltown: 2230 3rd Avenue *624-0556*
Open Monday through Friday for lunch and dinner.
Saturday and Sunday dinner only.

Middle-Eastern food. Reasonable prices. Falafil, baba ganooj, salads, lentil soups and very good hummus.

Julia's 14 Carrot Cafe
Eastlake: 2305 Eastlake Avenue E. *324-1442*
Open seven days a week for breakfast and lunch.
No dinner Sunday or Monday.

Julia's in Wallingford
Wallingford: 1714 N. 44th *633-1175*
Open seven days a week for breakfast, lunch and dinner.

Julia's bustles. Well-known for their breakfasts, Julia's is also the home of very good nutburgers. (Please, please try them.) Also pastas, some vegetarian soups, curried vegetables and homemade breads.

Kaleenka Russian Cafe
Downtown: 1933 1st Avenue *624-1278*
Open Monday through Saturday for lunch and dinner. Closed Sunday.

Small Russian cafe-like restaurant near the heart of downtown Seattle. Very high percentage of their compact menu is vegetarian, including cabbage or cheese piroshki, mashed potato or cheese pirogie (also known as Vareniky) and vegetarian borsht. Stop by on a Friday for potato cakes stuffed with mushrooms.

Kamalco
Capitol Hill: 414 E. Pine *323-7565*
Open seven days a week for dinner.

Besides falafil, hummus and baba ganooj and a great lentil soup, Kamalco has zarah (fried cauliflower in sauce) and stuffed grape leaves.

King's Chinese Restaurant
Lake City: 8055 Lake City Way N.E. *525-5464*
Open Tuesday through Sunday for dinner. Closed Monday.

This restaurant has a separate vegetarian menu. In addition, you can order brown rice or white rice, they don't use MSG in their food, and they cook with vegetable and sesame oil.

Kokeb Restaurant
South Capitol Hill: 926 12th Avenue *322-0485*
Open seven days a week for lunch and dinner. Saturday dinner only.

Ethiopian food. Try the misir wat (lentils with sauce), goman wat (cabbage, carrot and potato with sauce), the vegetarian combination, and the injera bread. They also make kickalacha, a yellow split-pea soup. Don't miss the all-you-can-eat Sunday brunch.

Lao Charearn
Downtown: 121 Prefontaine S. *223-9456*
Open seven days a week for lunch and dinner.

Laotian food is like Thai food. Lao Charearn has seven vegetarian selections. Some are: Tofu and vegetables, rice and vegetables, pad thai and, of course, spring rolls. Very reasonable prices.

Los Amigos
14707 Bothell Way N.E. *363-2500*
Open seven days a week for lunch and dinner.

A Mexican restaurant which does not put lard in its beans. They will also substitute beans for meat (many items are already beans only). Don't forget the cheese dishes, but pass on the flour tortillas (lard) and the rice and enchiladas, which are cooked in chicken stock and contain pieces of meat.

Marlene's Natural Foods
Federal Way: 2012 S. 320th *839-0933*
Open seven days a week for lunch.

The menu changes daily, but there are vegetarian and vegan soups, salads, and entrees every day. Deli service available. This place is ideal for vegans in south King County.

Mediterranean Kitchen
Near Seattle Center: 4 West Roy *285-6713*
Open seven days a week for dinner.

Lower Queen Anne Hill area. Middle-Eastern food. Falafil, hummus, baba ganooj and tabouleh always available. Try the lentil soup, too.

Meenar Restaurant
West Seattle: 4725 California S.W. *935-8993*
Open Tuesday through Friday for lunch and dinner.
Saturday and Sunday dinner only. Closed Monday.

Pakistani/Middle-Eastern/Indian food is on a menu which has a separate section for vegetarian entrees.

Morningtown
U-District: 4110 Roosevelt Way N.E. *632-6317*
Open seven days a week for lunch and dinner. Sunday dinner only.

Very relaxed pizza place with pizza, vegie sandwiches, Mexican and other ethnic foods. The menu is all vegetarian — that is, no anchovies, no pepperoni, etc. Foods are mostly organic and pastries are dairy, egg, sugar and salt-free. Will substitute tofu for pizza cheese. The home of the vegan pizza.

Natural Gourmet

Bainbridge: 345 Winslow Way *842-2759*
Open Monday through Saturday 10 a.m.-7 p.m. Sunday 12 noon-5 p.m.

A combination health/natural foods store and restaurant. They always have vegetarian sandwiches and salads and they usually have soup.

New Orleans Restaurant

Pioneer Square: 81 Yesler Way *622-2563*
Open Monday through Sunday for breakfast, lunch and dinner.

Here's something different for the Pacific Northwest — Creole food. Gumbo is a delicious okra soup, and the New Orleans Restaurant has a vegetarian variety. They also make a vegetarian eggplant dish and the traditional red beans and rice.

Panchito's

Pioneer Square: 1st Avenue and Cherry *343-9567*
Open seven days a week for lunch and dinner.

Mexican restaurant. Lardless refried beans, burritos and tacos.

Phoenecia Restaurant

Downtown-North: 100 Mercer Street *285-6739*
Open Tuesday through Sunday 5:30 p.m.-10:30 p.m.

Middle Eastern food. Vegetarian salads, appetizers and entrees. Meals have many, many courses.

Pleasant Peasant

Kirkland: 132 Central Way *827-5313*
Open Monday through Saturday for breakfast and lunch. Closed Sunday.

Cafeteria-style. Order at counter. Good selection of vegie soups, salads and sandwiches.

Rama House

Downtown: 2228 2nd Avenue *624-2931*
Open Monday through Friday for lunch and dinner.
Dinner only Saturday and Sunday.

Thai restaurant. Menu has special all-vegetarian section with a number of selections. Many rice, noodle and vegetable dishes with special peanut sauce. Unique desserts. Very friendly place.

You may count your intellect as superior to that of the animals; but in the light of the myriad Intelligences that move on a thousand planets, it is feeble and limited by your physical senses.

— Author Unknown

Rasa Malaysia
Downtown: 1514 Pike Place 624-8388
Open from lunch until 7 p.m. Closed Sunday.
U-District: 4300 University Way N.E. 545-7878
Open seven days a week for lunch and dinner.
Greenlake: 7802 E. Greenlake Drive 526-5864
Open seven days a week breakfast, lunch and dinner.

Malaysian food. Several noodle/rice and vegetable selections you can spice yourself with Malaysian sauces of your choosing. The Downtown and U-District locations are informal and nearly stand-up service and atmosphere. The Greenlake location has more tables. All three restaurants are inexpensive.

Ristorante Pony
Queen Anne: 621½ Queen Anne N. 283-8658
Open Tuesday through Saturday 11 a.m. until midnight;
Sunday brunch at 10 a.m., dinner 5-11 p.m.

Mediterranean specialties, many of which are vegetarian . . . lasagne, spanako-pita, soup, pasta . . .try the Arab salad. Sunday brunch offers many vegetarian selections. Staff is receptive to vegetarian requests.

Roosevelt Cafe
U-District: 4759 Roosevelt Way N.E. 632-7977
Open seven days a week for breakfast, lunch and dinner.

This restaurant is located below the Seven Gables Theatre. They offer several vegetarian main dishes (pasta, quiche), also omelets and baked eggs. All soups are made with vegetable stock, except for the chowder. Salads and fruit plates are on the menu, too. Their dessert selection is out of this world!

Sa Was Dee
Interbay area, between Queen Anne and Magnolia:
963 Elliott West 282-5707
Open Monday through Friday for lunch and dinner.
Saturday dinner only. Closed Sunday.

Thai restaurant. Look at the menu, pick a dish and substitute vegetables for animals. Sa Was Dee will usually oblige. Selection of noodles and tofu. Good peanut sauce.

Sabra Mediterranean
Downtown, across from Pike Place Market:
1916 Pike Place 682-1989
Open Monday through Saturday for lunch only.

Small place with take-out service and outdoor tables. Middle-Eastern food. Sandwiches served in pita bread. Three vegetarian soups per day. Entire menu is vegetarian except for tuna and provolone (rennet). Great selection of juices.

Sahara
U-District: 4752 University Way N.E. *527-5216*
Open Monday through Saturday for lunch and dinner.
Dinner only Sunday.

The U-District has a lot of Middle-Eastern restaurants. Here's another one that serves good vegetarian food.

Saigon
Downtown, across from Pike Place Market *622-6301*
Open Monday through Saturday from lunch until 6 p.m.

Small restaurant in the back of the Soames Dunn building. Menu has separate vegetarian section with tofu, noodles and soup. Very reasonable prices.

Seattle Center House
Formerly the Food Circus, Seattle Center Grounds
Open seven days a week

You know the Center House. It used to be the Food Circus. Restaurants galore. Well, look around this fast foods heaven and you'll find an interesting selection of vegetarian entrees.

Shalimar Restaurant
North U-District: 6409 Roosevelt Way N.E. *525-3950*
Open Monday through Saturday for dinner only.

Pakistani food (like Indian food). Menu has vegetable curries, soups and vegetarian appetizers. Menu also offers special vegetarian dinner.

Shezan Restaurant
Greenwood: 8733 Greenwood N. *783-2629*
Open Thursday through Sunday for dinner. Closed Monday.

Moderately-priced Indian restaurant. Traditional foods. Vegetarian appetizers. Both vegetable and potato curries available.

Silence Heart-Nest Restaurant
U-District: 5247 University Way N.E. *524-4008*
Open Monday through Saturday for lunch and early dinner.

There is so much Indian food which is vegetarian that it's only natural to expect an occasional all-vegetarian restaurant. This is one place where we don't have to recommend certain foods and not others. The entire menu is made-to-order for vegetarians. Soups, curries, those great Indian breads, side orders, salads and desserts. A good selection of vegan items. So relax and enjoy!

Silver Dragon
International District: 421 7th Avenue S. *622-4141*
Open seven days a week for lunch and dinner.

Most Chinese restaurants have one or two items, but the Silver Dragon has a separate menu for vegetarians which you must ask for. It has 30 dishes. The atmosphere is formal, service good. It's not inexpensive, but the food is well-prepared.

Sizzler Restaurant
Various Seattle locations
Open seven days a week for lunch and dinner.

Horrible name. Horrible name. Horrible name. Great salad bar. Great salad bar. Great salad bar.

Sound Food Restaurant and Bakery
Vashon Island *463-3565*
Open Wednesday through Monday for breakfast, lunch and dinner. Closed Tuesday.

Once the ferry deposits you on Vashon, resign yourself to staying a few hours. Sound Food has tempeh, baked vegetables and other sandwiches, soups and entrees. Want a great vegan breakfast (or lunch)? Try the scrambled tofu. Their Mexican food is made with lardless refried beans and (get this) lardless flour tortillas. Nice picture-window view, too. *The Minglement* health-food business is right next door.

Sound View Cafe
Pike Place Market *623-5700*
Open seven days a week for breakfast and lunch.

The Sound View Cafe used to be the Soup and Salad, if that jogs your memory. As their old name testifies, soup and salad (both vegetarian) are mainstays. And as the new name points out, you get a meal with a nice view. Sandwiches are also on the lunch menu, and on some days there's vegetarian chili. Have a breakfast of whole-grain pancakes, or eggs or muffins seven days a week.

Streamliner Diner
Bainbridge: 397 Winslow Way E. *842-8595*
Open seven days a week for breakfast and lunch.

Each day there's a vegetarian special like quiche, a soup or a salad. Also vegetarian sandwiches. Nice way to top off a ferry ride.

The Sunlight Cafe
North U-District: 6403 Roosevelt Way N.E. *522-9060*
Open seven days a week for breakfast, lunch and dinner.

The Sunlight offers an all-vegetarian and vegan menu. They have a good selection of sandwiches, salads, soups and breads. Dinner entrees are usually the same daily with one or two specials. They serve beer and wine and the desserts are excellent. An array of healthy beverages is available, too. Espresso is also served.

Taco Time
Various locations on greater roads everywhere.
Open seven days a week for lunch and dinner.

Fast food, Mexican-style. They will substitute beans for meat. No lard in beans or frying oil, but there's lard in the flour tortillas. Try the corn tortilla items.

Tanooki Sunflower Cafe
North U-District: 6311 Roosevelt Way N.E. 526-2935
Open Monday through Saturday for lunch and dinner. Sunday dinner only.

You can find a lot of Japanese restaurants in Seattle, but Japanese vegetarian food is another thing. Tanooki Sunflower has vegetarian yakisoba, tofu dishes, vegetarian humbow and a vegetarian kabob-type dish. Very reasonably priced.

Taqueria Mexico
U-District: 4226 University Way N.E. 633-5256
Open seven days a week for lunch and dinner.

Lardless refried beans. They will substitute beans for meat. Vegetarian burritos, tacos and tostadas. Avoid flour tortilla products (lard in flour tortillas).

Thai Palace
Near Denny Park, Seattle Center and the Elephant Car Wash
2224 8th Avenue 343-7846
Open Monday through Friday for lunch and dinner.
Dinner only Saturday and Sunday.

This medium-sized Thai restaurant has about ten vegetarian selections, including tofu dishes, pad thai and a cashew-broccoli plate.

Thai Restaurant
Near Seattle Center: 101 John 285-9000
Open Monday through Friday for lunch and dinner.
Dinner only Saturday and Sunday.

Seven vegetarian dishes. Eggplant, noodles, tofu curries and soups are available at this restaurant with the unusually straightforward name.

Thai Taste
West Seattle: 3247 California Avenue S.W. 937-6099
Open Tuesday through Sunday for dinner. Closed Monday.

Thai food. Mixed vegetable entree on menu. Very willing to make vegetarian substitutions.

Turkish Village
U-District: 5004 University Way N.E. 526-5061
Open Monday through Saturday for lunch and dinner. Closed Sunday.

Turkish Village seats about 35 people and serves vegan stuffed grape leaves, rice pilaf, bulgur salad and white bean salad. They also have jajik, a cold yogurt soup; and boreka, a spinach and cheese pastry.

Twelve Baskets Restaurant
Bellevue: 201 106th N.E. 455-3684
Open Monday through Friday for lunch and dinner.
Saturday breakfast, lunch and dinner. Closed Sunday.

Lunch menu has several salads, sandwiches and soups. In addition, vegetarian chili is always available. Dinner menu includes vegetable casserole and vegetable stews. All breads are homemade and wholegrain.

Vegetable Kingdom
Across from the Pike Place Market: 1906 Pike Place *343-9333*
Open Monday through Saturday for lunch.

Great name for a restaurant, right? Well, vegetables are the backbone of this establishment. Order your eight to ten steamed vegetables at the counter and choose from several sauces to top them with. Complete your meal with brown rice and wholegrain rolls. Eat inside (there are a few tables) or take your meal out and enjoy the Pike Place Market.

Viet-My Restaurant
Downtown: 129 Prefontaine Place S. *464-8681*
Open Monday through Saturday for lunch and dinner. Closed Sunday.

Tofu vegetable curry is very good. Vegetarian section on menu. Low prices.

Vietnam's Pearl Restaurant
Capitol Hill: 914 E. Pike *322-4080*
Open Monday through Saturday for lunch and dinner. Closed Sunday.

Vietnamese cuisine. Variety of vegetarian dishes, including mock meats (see our *Meat Substitutes* chapter), curries, soups and several tofu dishes. One of a small but growing number of Vietnamese restaurants in Seattle which seem to cater to vegetarian palates.

Wonder Freeze
Pike Place Market
Open Monday through Saturday.

Talk about your culinary pioneers. Danny, the owner of Wonder Freeze, has added vegetarian "hot dogs" to his menu. He did it especially for us, so go to the market and have a red hot. Wonder Freeze is across from the big news stand at the south entrance to the market.

Yak's Delicatessen
Fremont: 3424 Fremont N. *632-0560*
Open Monday through Saturday for lunch and dinner. Closed Sunday.

Inexpensive Asian food. Take-out type place with a few tables. A couple of vegetarian dishes, as well as vegetable humbow. Beautiful downtown Fremont.

Meat Substitutes

Soymeat

Soymeat (or soyameat) is an amazingly versatile food product that can increase the variety of a vegetarian's diet by leaps and bounds. It can be shaped and textured to look like just about anything, with mixed results. It's possible to find imitation hot dogs, hamburgers, turkey, chicken, cutlets, pâté, tuna, scallops and even steak.

Soyameat is not usually a vegan product; the primary way of texturing the soy protein in so many different ways is by mixing it with egg whites. Most of the various brands are canned or frozen; a few are dried, and once in a while they're fresh in the refrigerator case. But since the majority of brands are canned, they usually contain carbohydrates for body, and sodium (of course!) for taste. There are enough varieties available, fortunately, so that you can pick and choose and obtain "junky" soymeat or "healthy" soymeat to suit your tastes. There are even some vegan varieties available — you might have to look a bit harder at the labels though. In any case, "junky" or "healthy" soymeat is much healthier than meat, much lower in fat, cholesterol, additives and calories.

For a beginning vegetarian not normally inclined towards "health" foods, using soymeat to build meals around may be an easy way to start out. They can usually be substituted in ordinary meat-containing recipes, with little or no adaptation. Canned soymeats are usually packed in tasty juices that make an excellent substitute for meat juices in recipes.

Listed are some of the most palatable and easy-to-find varieties just to get you started; once you start looking, you can find almost anything you want.

The most accessible place to obtain soymeat is in the freezer of your local grocery store. Here lives Morningstar Farms: Grillers, Breakfast Links, and in some areas, Breakfast Strips (imitation bacon). If you ever crave a hamburger, a griller can be a pretty fair substitute, especially if you're careful not to overcook it. They can also be ground up and used in spaghetti, chili, tacos or stroganoff. Breakfast Links are probably the best imitation sausages found, and you can use and serve them in exactly the same ways as regular sausage, without the grease, cholesterol, or calories.

Of the canned varieties, Loma Linda, Worthington and Cedar Lake are the easiest to find in health-food stores. (Supermarkets are now beginning to introduce these products to their shelves, too.) Worthington has better texture and taste, and more variety, but also contains more additives and is made by a pharmaceutical company. Loma Linda foods are a bit more bland in taste and texture, but are more "pure." Cedar Lake foods are very bland, not very meatlike, but very nutritious — they just need a bit more creativity in the cooking process. Some good bets for starters are Worthington's franks, chili, "steak" strips, choplets, and imitation pressed "chicken," pressed "beef," and pressed "turkey" slices in gravy — good in sandwiches or hot with sauce. Loma Linda also makes good franks, "meat"balls, and imitation "chicken," along with a number of other protein products of not so identifiable tastes and textures. Both companies make good sandwich spreads.

Gluten

Gluten sounds icky. It must be named for the way it looks when it is sitting in a bowl before it is cooked — but it is one of the most useful meat substitutes available, and you can make it yourself. It comes from wheat flour — white or whole. It is the part of flour that makes dough stick together. Once separated from the starch and bran, it can be boiled or fried and will readily accept the spices and flavorings you prepare for it. Because of its sinewy, fibrous texture and because of some ancient Chinese Buddhist monks who experimented with combinations of spices to go with gluten, it is a meat substitute that tastes like meat.

Gluten takes a little bit of time to prepare, but not too much. If you don't have time, you can purchase cans of already seasoned gluten in many Chinese and Asian groceries (the International District is a great place for selection), and some health/natural-food stores. Gluten cannot substitute for every flavor and texture of meat, but it is versatile, it is obtained from common ingredients, and preparing it in the manner described in the "Basics" section (pp. 164-66) will also go a long way toward making its name less disagreeable, too.

There are frozen varieties of many of the above and more. You can find frozen vegetarian varieties of many classically non-vegetarian foods: lasagne, "veal" (!) parmesan, barbecue "beef," burritos, "fish" sticks, eggrolls, fried "chicken," and "tuna" salad. Dried soymeat is usually sold as TVP — textured vegetable protein. When reconstituted with water, it

---

Concommitant with the increases in American meat consumption is the appearance of famine in Third World countries . . . As Lappe points out, the cow is a protein factory in reverse. Twenty-one pounds of protein must be fed to a cow to make available one pound of protein for human consumption. Because of the large quantities of humanly edible protein being fed to animals and their inefficient conversion into protein for human consumption . . . in a single year 18 million tons of protein become inaccessible to man (sic). This is equivalent to 90% of the yearly world protein deficit.

— *Carol Adams*

ONE OF LIFE'S SIMPLE TRUTHS FINALLY DAWNS ON EMILY AT THE SUPERMARKET

can be substituted in many meat recipes. You can also find dried "ham" and "bacon" bits.

If soy products that resemble meat offend you, there are plenty of alternatives. Loma Linda and Cedar Lake in particular make several products that are pleasantly flavored and quite palatable and nutritious, and able to hold up the protein end of a meal without resembling anything in particular. For those who crave meat-type foods, but definitely want to avoid the real thing, soymeat might be ideal. Whatever your preferences, soymeat is a nutritious and good-tasting substitute for meat, and that's the important thing. Perhaps if more people were aware of the varieties available, we'd have more vegetarians.

You should note that soymeat is not inexpensive, except perhaps the dried varieties. The prices are comparable to, and occasionally higher than, any high-protein food. Additionally, the market for it is still fairly limited (to part of the vegetarian community, and to some on restricted diets for health reasons), so the price is higher due to low demand.

A few good places to shop for soymeat in the Seattle area are:

Mari-Don Healthway Natural Foods
1900 N. 45th (Wallingford)
Wide variety along with a good selection of rennetless cheeses.

Fred Meyer Health-Food Departments
(Various locations)
Cedar Lake products, various types of TVP.

GNC Nutrition Centers
(Various locations — see phone book for store nearest you)
Basic Worthington and Loma Linda; some frozen soymeat entrees, eggrolls and TVP.

Manna Mills
21705-66th West (Mountlake Terrace/Lynnwood)
Good selection of TVP. This is a good store for all of your vegetarian shopping.

The Seventh-Day Adventist Bookstore
20015 Bothell Way S.E. (Bothell)
Closed Saturday
Excellent selection of soymeat.

Almost any health-food store, no matter how small, has some selection of soymeat. If you don't see any, ask.

Recipes

CARNIVORES

KEEN NIGHT VISION
DRINK BY LAPPING
RASPY TONGUES
PERSPIRE BY PANTING
ACIDIC SALIVA
POINTED MOLARS FOR TEARING
UNDEVELOPED INCISORS
WELL-DEVELOPED CANINES
VERTICAL JAW ACTION ONLY
SIMPLE STOMACHS
ACIDIC DIGESTIVE JUICES TO BREAK DOWN ANIMAL TISSUE
SHORT INTESTINES
SMOOTH COLON
ACIDIC URINE

VEGETARIAN ANIMALS

POOR NIGHT VISION
DRINK BY SUCKING
SMOOTH TONGUES
PERSPIRE THRU PORES
ALKALINE SALIVA
BLUNT MOLARS FOR GRINDING
WELL-DEVELOPED INCISORS
UNDEVELOPED CANINES
VERTICLE & HORIZONTAL JAW ACTION
STOMACHS WITH COMPARTMENTS OR DUODENUMS
ALKALINE DIGESTIVE JUICES TO BREAK DOWN PLANT MATTER
LONG INTESTINES
CONVOLUTED COLONS
ALKALINE URINE

A Word About Protein

Before heading into the recipe section, we would like to address a concern many people have regarding whether or not their diet (specifically their vegetarian diet) provides them with all the protein their bodies need. The question that those of us who have been vegetarian for several years have been asked countless times, but with decreasing frequency through the years, is "How do you get your protein?" The reason we hear it with decreasing frequency is that this is an area in which there has been a great change — even a reversal — in general thinking. In the early 1970's, a vegetarian, particularly a vegan (who eats neither meat nor dairy products), was provided with many protein supplements and was warned against failing bones. If you ate dairy products, Mom and Dad, or even you yourself, often loaded your dinners with cheese, eggs, and milk to make up for what you "missed" with the meat you deleted. Also during those years, Frances Moore Lappe, within her very complete and well-regarded vegetarian reference book, *Diet for a Small Planet*, spelled out in detail the careful ways a vegetarian should combine his or her proteins so that his or her nutrition needs would surely be met. Times have changed, and most significantly for the vegetarian, so have theories about our protein needs. It now appears that about all we "miss" from not eating meat is the increased chance of being stricken with strokes, cancers, and heart disease. The incidence of those diseases has now been shown to be correlated with a meat-heavy diet! Furthermore, the Recommended Daily Allowance (RDA) for protein, though lowered throughout the years, is still being criticized for being higher than necessary.

In the new edition of *Diet for a Small Planet*, Frances Moore Lappe has reversed her own thinking about our protein needs and about the need for protein combining. She explains, "In the first edition, I emphasized that by

---

. . . meat-eating is exploitative not only of animals but of people as well, because it is predicated on overconsumption and misuse of land. It is a habit only the privileged are allowed to indulge." — Carol Adams
". . . the inedible complex: the political implications of Vegetarianism.

— *from the Oedible Complex:
Feminism and Vegetarianism*

---

combining protein you could create a quality as good as that of meat. I think I inadvertently contributed to a fixation on protein quality. I was concerned about being credible to the scientific establishment. I wanted doctors and nutritionists to use my book, which they have. I wanted to be scrupulous in my attention to detail and not do anything that would make them doubt me. In doing that, I didn't challenge enough the whole idea of how much protein we need."[1] In the new edition of her book, Lappé illustrates that unless a diet is heavily dependent on fruit or on certain tubers, or on junk food (refined flours, sugars, and fats), and a person is getting enough calories, then she or he is virtually assured of getting enough protein (though babies, young children and pregnant women need some special consideration, according to Lappé).[2]

We also would like to note that those posters promoting the four basic food groups that most of us grew up with (remember how they pushed high-protein diets?) were usually sponsored by industrial interests such as the National Dairy Council, McDonald's and DelMonte. Given that fact, we feel that it is wise that a vegetarian questions their validity.

So — as you probably have predicted — we do not subscribe to the notion that vegetarians have to count their grams and load up on protein. We feel that we are on safe ground when we say that there is enough protein in plant food to keep us healthy, and with the recipes we have included, no special effort was made to make them especially protein-packed. But we're also aware that there is a lot of conflicting information out about nutrition, and the last word will probably never be said. If you have questions, please do a little research on your own. We refer you particularly to *Diet for a Small Planet: 10th Anniversary Edition,* for the thorough research which addresses the global consequences of a meat-based versus a vegetarian diet. Even given the controversial nature of nutrition, as time goes on, and as more and more information comes to light, it appears that the lifestyle of the vegetarian need cause less and less personal worry. It is a lifestyle being associated not with sacrifice, but with health. Health for us, and what's good for all, health for the planet.

[1]Frances Moore Lappé, "Frances Moore Lappé: The Next Step," *Whole Life Times,* July/August 1984, p. 20.

[2]Frances Moore Lappé, *Diet for a Small Planet: 10th Anniversary Edition,* (New York,: Ballantine Books, 1982), p. 162.

Breakfasts

When looking for breakfast or brunch ideas don't ignore bread and dessert recipes. Pumpkin bread, apple cake and banana bread are just a few of the not-too-sweet baked goods which are tastier and more nutritious than many traditional sweet breakfast pastries. Or try vegan biscuits from the bread section served with one of the gravy recipes we have listed.

Hash browns are a hearty addition to your breakfast menu — especially good topped with imitation bacon bits.

A powdered mix called Tofu Scramble® is available at most health food stores. It turns a pound of tofu into a concoction to rival the yummiest scrambled eggs. And don't forget oatmeal or grits topped with Mocha Mix® as a filling way to start the day.

Breakfast Apple Cobbler *

8 to 10 servings

8 medium tart apples, cored,
  sliced and peeled
¾ c. melted margarine
2 c. natural mixed cereal with fruit
  and/or nuts (granola type)

1 c. brown sugar
dash cinnamon
1 Tbsp. lemon juice
½ tsp. grated lemon rind

Place apples in crock pot. Add remaining ingredients and mix. Cook on high 3 hours or low 6-10 hours. Serve with non-dairy topping.

Our livestock and poultry consume 97% of our nation's legumes, 90% of its corn, 64% of barley, 88% of its oats . . . Yet meat accounts for only 20% of our diet!

— from "Vegetarianism for a World of Plenty"
Moneysworth, March 1979

Note: An asterisk after the recipe title means the recipe is (or can be made) vegan, using no eggs or dairy products.

Fresh Fruit Smoothie*

Serves 1

½ ripe banana, peeled
6 large strawberries, tops removed

¼ c. blueberries
orange juice

Place fruit in blender container. Add just enough orange juice to cover fruit. Cover and blend on high until smooth. Pour into a glass and serve.

This beverage makes a delicious quick breakfast or snack. Vary it by adding other fruits or using different juices, or by adding 1 Tbsp. wheat germ before blending. The volume increases while blending, so if making smoothies for a crowd be sure to leave extra space at the top of the blender container.

Fried Corn Cakes*

Serves 4 to 6

2½ c. water
1 tsp. salt

1¼ c. corn meal
1 c. cold water

In a large saucepan, bring 2½ c. water and salt to a boil over medium-high heat. Mix corn meal with 1 c. cold water and add slowly to boiling water, stirring. Cook over low heat 5 minutes, stirring constantly. Pour into a greased loaf pan. Chill 1 hour, or cover and chill overnight.

Slice about ½-inch thick and fry on a greased griddle over medium-high heat, flipping when the first side is golden. Serve hot with syrup.

Granola*

3 quarts

4 c. rolled old-fashioned oats
1½ c. coconut
1½ c. sunflower nuts
½ c. sesame seeds
1½ c. chopped nuts (peanuts, cashews, pecans or almonds)
½ c. whole wheat flour

½ c. sliced almonds
1¾ c. honey
¾ c. oil
2 tsp. vanilla
1 Tbsp. cinnamon (optional)
1 c. chopped dates
1 c. chopped raisins

In a large bowl, mix together the oats, coconut, sunflower nuts, sesame seeds, chopped nuts, wheat germ, whole wheat flour and almonds.

In a saucepan, mix the honey, oil, vanilla and cinnamon. Heat over low heat, stirring frequently, until well-blended and very warm. Pour over dry ingredients. Stir to mix thoroughly. Spread mixture on 2 ungreased cookie sheets.

Bake at 300° for 20 minutes, or until light golden, stirring often. Watch closely to prevent burning. Remove from the oven and stir in dates and raisins. Cool completely before storing in covered containers.

Potato Pancakes*

12 pancakes

2 medium-large potatoes, scrubbed but not peeled, and coarsely grated (about 4 c. shredded)	¼ tsp. salt
	1 tsp. paprika
	1/3 c. chopped onion
3 Tbsp. flour	several shakes black pepper

Place shredded potatoes in a strainer and shake well to drain off excess water. Mix with remaining ingredients.

In a large frying pan heat ¼ c. margarine over medium-high heat. With cupped hands shape the mixture into patties, using about 1/3 c. potato mixture per patty. Press hands together firmly to squeeze out excess water. Flatten to ½-¾ inch thick in center.

Place gently in pan. Fry until golden, then carefully turn over to cook the other side. Add more margarine as necessary to prevent sticking. If patties are too thick they may not cook in the middle, so test the first one to make sure it's completely done. These pancakes can also be cooked in oil, but the margarine adds flavor. Serve hot.

Scrambled Denver Tofu*

Serves 4 to 6

2 lbs. tofu, crumbled into large pieces (firm tofu works best)	1 tsp. soy sauce or tamari
	½ tsp. salt
1 medium onion, chopped	½ tsp. turmeric
1 green pepper, chopped	½ tsp. garlic powder
¼ c. margarine	freshly ground black pepper to taste
3 shakes hot pepper sauce	

Place tofu in colander and shake repeatedly to drain well. Let drain while you saute onions and green pepper in margarine over medium-high heat until soft. Add tofu. Add hot pepper sauce, soy sauce and spices. Continue cooking on medium-high, stirring frequently, until tofu is hot, about 10 minutes. If liquid remains in pan, cook longer or serve with slotted spoon.

This is a tasty and healthy scrambled egg substitute, and makes terrific Denver Sandwiches served on bread with margarine and tofu mayonnaise (or regular mayonnaise).

Seven Grain Cereal*

2 Servings

2 c. water
½ c. seven grain cereal
dash salt

Bring water to a boil in an oven-proof saucepan. Stir in cereal and salt. Cover immediately and place in oven on "warm" overnight. Cereal will be just right in the morning.

Soymilk Pancakes*

6 medium pancakes

2 Tbsp. sugar
1½ tsp. baking powder
1 tsp. salt
1½ c. flour (white and/or whole wheat)

1½ c. soymilk (you can use water or liquid non-dairy creamer for up to half the liquid)

Combine all ingredients, stirring briefly with a whisk. You may need to add more liquid if you use whole wheat flour — the batter should be pourable.

Heat a skillet or griddle with oil or margarine until skillet hisses when you sprinkle a couple drops of water on it. Pour batter on skillet, cook until top of pancake bubbles, then turn over.

We have no right to inflict suffering and death on another living creature unless there is some unavoidable necessity for it, and then we ought all of us to feel what a horrible thing it is to cause suffering and death out of mere thoughtlessness.
— Albert Schweitzer

Tofu Waffles with Fruit*

About 4 waffles or 8 pancakes

1½ c. flour, white or whole wheat
1 Tbsp. baking powder
pinch nutmeg
3 Tbsp. cornstarch
¼ lb. tofu

1 tsp. vanilla
1½ c. water
1 Tbsp. honey
¾ c. melted margarine

Combine dry ingredients in a large bowl. Blend tofu and liquid ingredients in a blender until smooth. Add to the dry mixture and stir well. Bake in a preheated waffle iron until golden brown. Serve with fresh sliced fruit and non-dairy whipped topping.

This recipe may be used as a pancake batter by reducing margarine from ¾ c. to ¼ c. and increasing water to 2 c. Cook on an oiled skillet.

"I FEEL SO COUPED UP TODAY..."

Breads

Good breads can play a substantial role in an interesting, versatile, cruelty-free diet, and what better way to enjoy bread than to eat the fresh, home-made variety?

The word "yeast" must have originally meant "work and wait," because you do a lot of that with yeast-type breads. But as all the bread-making books inevitably tell you, it is worth it. Moreover, making your own bread gives you control over what goes into it, so you no longer have to read bread wrappers to avoid lard, whey, eggs, and the fine print chemicals that help your body grow strong twelve different ways.

*Banana Bread**

1 loaf

1 c. sugar	1½ tsp. baking soda
3 Tbsp. oil	1½ tsp. baking powder
1 tsp. vanilla	½ c. orange juice
½ tsp. salt	2 large or 3 small very ripe bananas,
2 c. flour	mashed (about 1½ c.)

Combine all ingredients and mix well. Spread in a greased and floured loaf pan.

Bake at 325° for 1 hour, or until a toothpick inserted in the center comes out clean.

People who are concerned about killing plants should definitely become vegetarians because they will consume only a small fraction of the plants that are fed to livestock to yield an equivalent amount of animal food.

— Veg. Information Service

Note: An asterisk after the recipe title means the recipe is (or can be made) vegan, using no eggs or dairy products.

Biscuit Mix*

9 cups

8 c. flour
1/3 c. baking powder
2 tsp. salt

3 Tbsp. sugar
1 c. solid vegetable shortening

Mix flour, baking powder, salt and sugar in a large bowl. Cut in 1 c. shortening, using two dinner knives or a pastry blender, until a very fine consistency is reached. Store in a tightly covered container at room temperature for a few days, or refrigerate for up to a month.

To use, mix 1 c. of this mixture with ¼ to 1/3 c. water. Knead on a floured board for a few minutes and roll out about ½-inch thick on a floured board. Cut into desired shapes and place on an ungreased cookie sheet.

Bake at 425° until light golden, about 8-10 minutes. Do not overbake.

For drop biscuits, omit kneading. Drop onto a cookie sheet and bake as above.

Fast Oat-Wheat Bread*

2 loaves

1½ c. dry oatmeal
3 pkgs. baking yeast
4 c. warm water
3 Tbsp. honey
¼ c. honey (or part molasses)

1 Tbsp. salt
¼ c. oil
1/3 c. soy grits
5 c. whole wheat flour
1 c. whole wheat flour

Warm the oatmeal in the oven.

Dissolve yeast in warm water with 3 Tbsp. honey. Let stand 10 minutes (until it bubbles) in a warm location. Then let stand an additional 10 minutes. Add the ¼ c. honey, salt and oil. Next, add the warm oatmeal. Let stand for 2-3 minutes. Add wheat germ, soy grits and 5 c. flour.

Using the additional 1 c. flour if necessary, turn out onto a floured board and knead well until elastic. Divide dough and shape into 2 loaves. Place in two large greased loaf pans.

Bake at 275° for 15 minutes, then increase temperature to 350° and bake an additional 35 minutes.

The oatmeal may be omitted and replaced with 1½-2 c. of any type of flour.

Flour Tortillas*

6-8 tortillas

2 c. flour
¼ c. solid vegetable shortening
1½ tsp. salt

1 tsp. baking powder
2/3 c. warm water

Mix all ingredients. Pinch off enough dough to make the desired size of tortilla, and roll out to correct size and shape. Cook over medium-high heat in an ungreased fry pan, 15-30 seconds per side. Place separately on paper towels or clean paper sacks to cool.

Orange Corn Bread*

1 loaf

¼ c. honey
2 Tbsp. oil
1 c. water or orange juice
1 tsp. orange extract

1 tsp. grated orange rind
1 Tbsp. baking powder
1¾ c. corn meal
¼ c. whole wheat flour

Combine the honey, oil, water, orange extract and orange rind in a medium bowl and stir until smooth. Add the remaining ingredients and mix just until blended. Pour the batter into a well-greased loaf pan.

Bake at 400° for 25 minutes, or until a toothpick inserted in the center comes out clean. Cool for 5 minutes in the pan, then remove.

Pumpkin Bread*

4 loaves

4 c. sugar
1 c. oil
1½ 29-oz. cans pumpkin, or
   1 29-oz. plus 1 15-oz. can
5 c. flour
1 tsp. salt

4 tsp. baking soda
2 tsp. cloves
4 tsp. cinnamon
1 tsp. nutmeg
1 c. raisins
1 c. chopped walnuts

Mix sugar, oil and pumpkin. Sift dry ingredients and stir into pumpkin mixture. Add raisins and nuts and mix well. Divide batter in 4 well-greased loaf pans.

Bake at 350° for 1 hour.

Tofu Apple Nut Bread*

1 loaf

1 c. crumbled tofu, well drained (½ lb.)
2 c. apple butter (1 15-oz. jar)
5 Tbsp. oil
¼ c. honey
rind of 1 lemon, grated
1 Tbsp. lemon juice

½ tsp. cinnamon
¼ tsp. salt
2 c. whole wheat flour
1½ tsp. baking soda
1 c. raisins
½ c. chopped walnuts

Combine the tofu, apple butter, oil, honey, lemon rind, lemon juice and cinnamon in a blender and blend until smooth. Sift together the salt, flour and baking soda. Combine with apple butter mixture and stir well. Stir in raisins and walnuts and pour into a greased 9-inch ring pan or loaf pan.

Bake at 350° for 50 minutes, or until a toothpick inserted in the center comes out clean. Remove from pan after cooling for 5 minutes.

Vegan Whole Wheat Bread*

2 loaves

2 envelopes dry baking yeast
3 c. hot tap water (not over 130°)
¼ c. black molasses

1/3 c. honey
6 c. stoneground whole wheat flour
1 Tbsp. sea salt

Dissolve yeast in water, then stir in molasses and honey until well mixed. Slowly stir in all but a cupful of the flour. Knead for 10 minutes, using the remaining flour on the board and hands to prevent sticking. Cover with a towel and let rise in a warm place until doubled in volume.

Punch down. Let rise a second time to double in size again.

Punch down once more and quickly knead into a ball (just a few kneads). Separate into two equal pieces and shape into loaves. Set in ungreased loaf pans. Then set the two pans in a sink of warm water, 3 inches deep, and let rise a third time, until double in size. This makes the dough equal density throughout.

Bake at 400° for 10 minutes, then reduce heat to 375° and continue baking for 35 minutes, or until a knife inserted in the center comes out clean.

Salads

Do you think of a salad as the introduction to lunch or dinner? It can fill other roles as well. Many of the recipes in this section are for salads filling enough to be the center of a meal. Try the taco salad with rice on the side; or a pasta salad, bread and soup.

Others, like eggless egg salad, are tasty sandwich fillings. Marinated mushrooms can double as an appetizer. Most of these salads will travel well to work or to a picnic. The dressing should be packed separately and applied just before eating.

The following recipes may dramatically increase your list of possible salad ingredients from the typical lettuce and tomato fare. You can probably invent other imaginative combinations. Eat salads often — they are a great source of fiber and vitamins.

The salad dressings we have listed will be at their most flavorful if made ahead, refrigerated for at least four hours, and then taken out of the refrigerator so that they can warm up for about 15 minutes before serving.

Barley Raisin Salad*

4 to 6 servings

Salad:
3 c. cooked barley
½ c. raisins
½ c. chopped toasted almonds
½ c. finely chopped celery
½ c. coarsely grated carrot

Dressing:
¼ c. lemon juice
1/3 c. olive oil
2 Tbsp. soy sauce or tamari

Combine and mix ingredients

Mix all salad ingredients thoroughly, breaking up any raisin clusters. Dress salad well before serving.

Note: An asterisk after the recipe title means the recipe is (or can be made) vegan, using no eggs or dairy products.

Cashew Romaine Salad*

4 servings

Salad:
1 head romaine lettuce, rinsed, dried, and broken into bite-size pieces
½ c. salted roasted cashews
¼ c. thinly sliced red onion
½ c. cooked or canned garbanzo beans, rinsed and drained

Dressing:
2 Tbsp. cider vinegar
2 tsp. prepared Dijon mustard
½ tsp. salt
⅛ tsp. freshly ground pepper
pinch cumin
pinch cardamom
¼ to ⅜ c. light olive oil or salad oil

Combine salad ingredients. Toss with dressing just before serving.

Cherry Fruit Bowl*

4 to 6 servings

Salad:
1 c. maraschino cherries
1 13½-oz. can pineapple chunks
1 11-oz. can mandarin orange segments
1 tart apple, cored and cut into wedges
1½ c. seedless green grapes

Lemon-Orange Dressing:
½ c. light corn syrup or sugar
1½ Tbsp. cornstarch
½ c. unsweetened pineapple juice
1 tsp. grated lemon peel
1 tsp. grated orange peel
2 Tbsp. lemon juice
2 Tbsp. orange juice

Salad: Chill all fruit, reserving half the mandarin orange segments and half the cherries. Just before serving, drain pineapple, oranges, and cherries thoroughly. Place in large bowl. Add grapes and apple wedges. Pour dressing over fruit. Toss until well-coated. Arrange reserved cherries and orange segments alternately in a ring on top of the salad. Two dressings are good with this salad: Lemon-Orange Dressing or Sour Cream Dressing (following Strawberry Fruit Bowl recipe).

Dressing: Mix first two ingredients in small saucepan. Stir in pineapple juice. Cook, stirring constantly, until mixture thickens and boils. Boil for one minute, stirring. Remove from heat, stir in remaining ingredients, and chill.

To my mind the life of a lamb is no less precious than that of a human being . . . I hold that, the more helpless a creature, the more entitled it is to protection by man from the cruelty of man.

— Gandhi

Marinated Garbanzos*

4 to 6 servings

4 c. cooked, drained garbanzo beans
   (canned will be fine)
½ c. vinaigrette-type salad dressing

½ c. chopped parsley
¼ c. chili sauce
1 tsp. oregano

Combine all ingredients and chill several hours. Garnish with sliced tomatoes and additional parsley.

Marinated Mushroom Salad*

6 to 8 servings

1½ lb. fresh mushrooms
2 6-oz. jars marinated artichoke hearts
¼ c. pine nuts

choice of herbs:
   tarragon, basil, parsley and/or
   rosemary

Wash mushrooms. combine in a medium bowl with artichoke hearts and their marinade. Add pine nuts. Add approximately one teaspoon of one or more of the above herbs and stir well. Chill several hours before serving. This will work well as an appetizer.

Marinated Salad*

6 to 8 servings

2 bunches broccoli, stalks peeled
   and thinly sliced, tops cut into
   florets, about 3 cups
½ head cauliflower, thinly sliced

1 4-oz. can mushrooms, drained
1 2-oz. jar pimientos, diced
2 large carrots, thinly sliced
1 c. Italian or oil & vinegar dressing

Combine all ingredients. Marinate in dressing for at least 10 hours, stirring several times.

Linda and I are vegetarians mainly because we really love animals. And if we're driving behind a truckload of sheep, being sheep farmers ourselves, we know where those sheep are going. And I think I really don't want to get behind that kind of thing myself.

— Paul McCartney
(No animals are killed on the McCartney farm)

Pasta Primavera Salad*

6 to 8 servings

Salad:
8 oz. dry pasta (shells, spirals or other interesting shapes), cooked and cooled
8 asparagus spears, trimmed of tough ends and cut into 1½" lengths
1½ c. broccoli florets
1½ c. frozen peas, thawed but not cooked
¾ c. tofu mayonnaise or regular mayonnaise
optional (for garnish):
    10 cherry tomatoes, halved
    ¼ lb. fresh spinach leaves, washed and dried

Pesto Dressing:
2 c. fresh basil leaves
1 clove garlic, minced
¼ c. walnuts
¼ c. olive oil
1 tsp salt

Steam broccoli and asparagus until just barely tender and still bright green. Rinse with cold water. Combine with pasta, peas and mayonnaise and stir well. Whir dressing ingredients in blender. Add dressing a little at a time until salad is dressed to your taste.

To garnish: Arrange spinach leaves around edge of shallow bowl or platter. Arrange pasta in center, with leaves as border. Top with cherry tomatoes.

Pasta Salad*

6 servings

4 oz. (about 1 c.) dried salad macaroni
  or other medium size pasta
1 6-oz. jar marinated artichoke hearts
¼ lb. small mushrooms
1 c. cherry tomatoes, halved

1 c. medium sized pitted ripe
  olives, sliced
1 Tbsp. chopped parsley
¼ tsp. dry basil
salt and pepper

Cook macaroni according to package directions. Drain well, rinse with cold water and drain again. Add artichokes and their liquid, mushrooms, cherry tomatoes, olives, parsley and basil. Toss gently. Cover and refrigerate at least 4 hours or until the next day. Before serving season with salt and pepper to taste.

Potato Salad*

8 servings

Salad:
6 medium potatoes, washed but
   not peeled
¼ c. chopped onion
1 4-oz. can chopped black olives
1 tsp. salt
optional additions:
   chopped radishes, celery,
   green onion or pimientos,
   or sliced almonds

Dressing:
¼ c. oil
½ c. tofu mayonnaise or
   regular mayonnaise
1 Tbsp. lemon juice
¼ tsp. oregano
¼ tsp. dry mustard
1 tsp. sugar or honey
¼ tsp. paprika
pinch of thyme
1 clove garlic, crushed, or
   ¼ tsp. garlic powder

Cover potatoes with water in a saucepan. Boil for one-half hour. Drain, cool and dice. Add onions, olives and salt. Combine dressing ingredients, pour over salad and mix well. Chill.

Spinach Salad*

10 to 12 servings

Salad:
2-3 bunches of fresh spinach
   (use small whole leaves if possible)
2-3 Tbsp. artifical bacon bits
1 8-oz. can sliced water chestnuts, drained
1 c. fresh bean sprouts
½ lb. fresh mushrooms, sliced thin

Dressing:
1 c. oil
¼ c. cider vinegar
1 Tbsp. dried chopped onion
1/3 c. catsup
¾ c. sugar

Arrange all ingredients in a large bowl or on individual plates. Just before serving, top with dressing.

We are custodians and patrons of a massive art gallery called NATURE. It is time we took down the sign which reserves a corner for those who enjoy the sound of ripping canvas. There are better ways to enjoy art, and it's about time we learned.

— Hope Sawyer Buyukmihci
Famed vegetarian naturalist,
author and illustrator

Spinach Salad Surprise*

4 servings

Salad:
1 large bunch spinach
  torn into bite-size pieces
1 red apple, chopped
2 green onions, chopped
½ c. toasted sliced almonds
2 Tbsp. artificial bacon bits

Dressing:
¼ c. oil
3 Tbsp. red wine vinegar
dash each salt and pepper
1 tsp. sugar
¼ tsp. dry mustard
Combine and mix ingredients

Combine in large salad bowl. Add dressing (above) and toss.

Strawberry Fruit Bowl

6 to 8 servings

Salad:
1 c. strawberries, halved
4 medium oranges, peeled and
  sectioned
3 medium bananas
1½ c. seedless green grapes

Sour Cream Dressing:
½ c. sour cream
1 Tbsp. sugar
1 Tbsp. orange juice
¼ c. flake coconut

Salad: Peel bananas and slice into a medium bowl. Cover completely with half the strawberries, half the oranges, and all of the grapes. (Reserve remaining strawberries and oranges for garnish). Cover bowl and chill. Just before serving, pour dressing over fruit; toss until well coated. Arrange reserved strawberries and oranges alternately in a ring on top of the salad. Two dressings are good with this salad: Sour Cream Dressing or Lemon-Orange Dressing (see Cherry Fruit Bowl recipe).

Dressing: Put all ingredients in blender and blend until smooth.

If our goal is to live in a world without oppression, where does meat-eating fit into this vision?

— Carol Adams

Tabouli Salad*

4 to 6 servings

1 c. uncooked bulgur wheat
2 c. boiling water
1½ tsp. salt
⅛ tsp. freshly ground black pepper
¼ c. fresh lemon juice
½ c. green onions, chopped, including tops
3 medium tomatoes, chopped

½ c. parsley, chopped
2-3 Tbsp. fresh mint, crumbled
  (can use dried)
½ c. sliced black olives
1 tsp. garlic, minced
¼ c. olive oil

Begin at least 3 hours before serving. Pour boiling water over bulgur, and allow to soak. After at least one hour, drain off any extra water that has not soaked in. Add remaining ingredients and stir to blend well. Adjust mint, lemon juice, garlic and salt to taste. Chill at least 2 hours.

Taco Salad

6 to 8 servings

1 16-oz. can kidney beans
1 pkg. taco seasoning mix
1 large onion, chopped
4 medium tomatoes, chopped
1 avocado, peeled and chopped
1 head lettuce, chopped

6 oz. tortilla chips, crumbled
8 oz. cheddar cheese, grated
1 c. (8 oz. bottle) of one of the
  following dressings: sour cream with
  onion, ranch or thousand island

Place kidney beans in skillet with taco seasoning and cook according to directons on package. Cool. Toss all ingredients together.

Optional: Layer all ingredients in a 9x13-inch pan and top with dressing and cheese.

Three Bean Salad*

6 to 8 servings

1 16-oz. can green beans, drained, or
  1 10-oz. pkg. frozen green beans, cooked
1 16-oz. can garbanzo beans, drained
1 16-oz. can red kidney beans, drained
½ c. chopped green pepper
½ c. chopped red onion

½ c. oil
½ c. cider vinegar
1/3 c. sugar
1 tsp. salt
½ tsp. pepper

Mix all ingredients and chill overnight.

Tofu "Egg Salad"*

4 servings

¾ lb. firm tofu, diced, drained and gently blotted dry (1½-2 c.)
3 minced scallions (whites and greens)
2 stalks celery, chopped
1 small can (2¼ oz.) sliced black olives, drained
½ tsp. prepared mustard
1½ c. tofu mayonnaise or regular mayonnaise
salt and freshly ground pepper to taste

Combine tofu with scallions, celery and olives in a medium bowl. Mix gently. Add tofu mayonnaise and mustard and mix again. Season to taste and mix again. Chill and serve in pita bread with lettuce.

Wilted Lettuce or Spinach Salad*

4 servings

1 large head lettuce or
  1 large bunch spinach
1 medium onion, chopped
¼ c. oil
2 Tbsp. flour

¾ c. water
¼ c. vinegar
3 Tbsp. sugar or honey
⅛ tsp. salt
croutons

Cut or tear lettuce or spinach into strips. Place in a large bowl.

Heat oil in skillet and fry onions until clear. Stir in flour. Add water, vinegar, sugar and salt. Bring to a boil. Pour over greens while hot, in order to wilt them. Top with croutons.

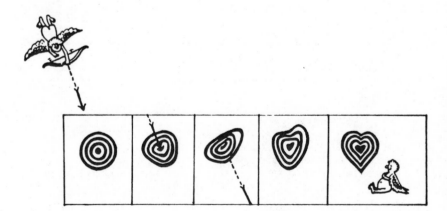

Salad Dressings

*French Dressing**

1 pint

1/3 c. cider or wine vinegar
2 tsp. minced onion
1 clove garlic, peeled
5 whole peppercorns
½ tsp. salt

1 tsp. paprika
½ tsp. dry mustard
¼ tsp. dill seed
¼ tsp. celery seed

Blend above ingredients thoroughly in a blender. Then, with blender running, add slowly, one at a time:

2 tsp. sugar
½ c. oil
½ c. water

There is no right to life in any society on Earth today, nor has there been at any former time. We raise farm animals for slaughter; destroy forests; pollute rivers and lakes until no fish can live there; hunt deer and elk for sport, leopards for their pelts, and whales for dog food; entwine dolphins, gasping and writhing, in great tuna nets; and club seal pups to death for 'population management.' All these beasts and vegetables are as alive as we. What is protected in many human societies is not life, but human life.

— from **Dragons of Eden**
by Carl Sagan

Note: An asterisk after the recipe title means the recipe is (or can be made) vegan, using no eggs or dairy products.

Lemon-Herb Dressing*

1 pint

½ c. lemon juice
½ c. chopped green onion,
   including tops
2 tsp. sugar
1 tsp. oregano
½ tsp. dry mustard

2 tsp. basil
1 tsp. celery seed
1 tsp. dill seed
¼ tsp. rosemary
pinch cayenne

Blend all ingredients in a blender, then add:

½ tsp. tamari or soy sauce
½ c. salad oil

Blend again.

Creamy Herbal Dressing*

1 pint

Substitute ½ lb. (1 c. mashed) drained tofu for the lemon juice in Lemon-Herbal Dressing, above.

Poppy Seed Dressing*

3 cups

¾ c. honey or sugar
2 tsp. mustard seed
1 tsp. salt

2/3 c. cider vinegar
½ c. onion
3 Tbsp. poppy seeds

Blend all ingredients in a blender. Slowly, with blender on low, add:

1½ c. oil

Soy Mayonnaise*

1 quart

1 c. soymilk
1 Tbsp. sugar
2 c. vegetable oil

1/3 c. Italian olive oil (or vegetable oil)
2 tsp. salt
2 Tbsp. white vinegar

Blend milk and sugar in a blender. With blender running, drizzle in oils, vinegar, and salt. Mixture will stiffen. Stir to mix well. Refrigerate.

Tofu Mayonnaise*

1½ cups

1 c. tofu
2-4 Tbsp. oil
1 tsp. salt
4 Tbsp. vinegar

2 Tbsp. sugar
⅛ tsp. garlic powder
pinch black pepper

Blend ingredients until smooth, using a rubber scraper on the sides of the blender. Chill. This makes an excellent mayonnaise substitute in sandwiches, dips, or salads.

Reprinted with permission from *The Farm Vegetarian Cookbook*.

Tofuvocado Dressing*

1 quart

1 pkg. smooth tofu
3 soft avocados
½ onion, cut in chunks
3 cloves garlic, minced

1 Tbsp. lemon juice
1 Tbsp. taco sauce (mild)
Salt

Break tofu into chunks. Place in blender a little at a time, whirling. Blend until smooth. Add avocados a quarter at a time, blending smooth after each addition; repeat with onion. Add garlic, lemon juice, and taco sauce. Whirl. Salt to taste.

Yogurt-Lime Dressing

1½ cups

2 Tbsp. prepared mustard
5 Tbsp. oil
1 c. plain yogurt

juice from ½ lime
1 clove garlic, minced

Place mustard in a medium mixing bowl. Slowly add oil, stirring constantly in the same direction to prevent separation. Add yogurt; mix well. Add lime juice and garlic and mix again. Add salt and pepper to taste if desired.

Sandwiches and Appetizers

Many bean spreads and vegetable-based dips work equally well served as appetizers with fresh vegetables or crackers, or as sandwich fillings.

Sandwiches packed for work or school brown-bag lunches will taste fresher if watery ingredients, such as tomato slices or pineapple, or ingredients sensitive to air exposure, such as bananas, are packed separately and added just before eating. Toasting bread before assembling the sandwich adds a little extra chewiness and also keeps the sandwich from becoming soggy between the morning commute and lunchtime.

Below are just a few quick and tasty possibilities to get you started thinking in terms other than ham-and-cheese, spam-and-cheese, bologna-and-cheese...

- Cold baked beans topped with thin slices of tomato or onion.

- Peanut butter with raisins and banana slices.

- Thin slices of well-drained and pressed firm tofu topped with tomato, olives, sprouts and a bit of salad dressing. Margarine on the bread helps prevent sogginess. This is even better with fried tofu slices.

- Cucumber and tomato slices on soft bread with margarine and a little tofu mayonnaise.

- Sweet, mild onion slices with margarine.

- A late summer treat: thick slices of fresh ripe tomato on whole wheat bread with margarine. Carry the tomato whole, to slice just before lunch. Pack the bread with margarine sides face-to-face.

- Garbanzo bean spread with sweet pickles.

- Imitation bacon bits, lettuce and tomato on toast with tofu mayonnaise. This non-BLT packs well.

- Hawaiian sandwich: well-drained crushed pineapple, artificial bacon bits, green pepper slices on toast with tofu mayonnaise. Added tomato slices or lettuce leaves are good, too.

- Mashed avocado, mango slices and alfalfa sprouts.

- Cooked lentils (simmer 1 c. dry lentils in 2½ c. salted water for 40 minutes, or until soft, then drain well and season with salt and pepper) with sliced tomato and onions.

- Mashed avocado, finely grated cabbage and radishes, chopped green onions and alfalfa sprouts with tofu mayonnaise.
- Mashed avocado, tomato slices, chopped unsalted peanuts and alfalfa sprouts.
- Salad with dressing and sunflower seeds, to pack into pocket bread just before eating.

Basic Dip*

Starting with tofu mayonnaise or regular mayonnaise as a base, you can make a quick dip by adding any number of herbs, seasonings or shredded vegetables. Try:

- fresh or dried dill weed
- curry powder with a little dried mustard and brown sugar
- an abundance of finely chopped green onion
- chopped pimiento or onion broth concentrate
- Lipton Onion Soup mix (1 envelope to 2 c. tofu mayonnaise)
- curry powder, garlic, lemon juice and cayenne

These are best if chilled several hours before serving.

Some Like It Hot Dip*

½ cup

½ c. catsup
½-1 Tbsp. horseradish

Mix together. Serve at room temperature as a dip for deep-fried vegetables (cauliflower and mushrooms are wonderful).

It takes 1,000 gallons of water to produce 1 McDonald's Hamburger.

— from "Vegetarianism for a World of Plenty"
Moneysworth, March 1979

Note: An asterisk after the recipe title means the recipe is (or can be made) vegan, using no eggs or dairy products.

Caramel Corn*

6-8 quarts

2 c. brown sugar
1 c. margarine
½ c. light corn syrup
1 tsp. salt

1 tsp. vanilla
½ tsp. baking soda
6-8 quarts popped corn
12 oz. mixed nuts or peanuts, optional

In a 2-quart saucepan bring sugar, margarine and syrup to a boil. Boil 5 minutes, stirring constantly, over medium heat. Do not overboil. Add salt, vanilla and soda, stirring after each. Pour over the popped corn in a large bowl. Stir to distribute the coating well, then add nuts and stir again. Place on 2 large cookie sheets.

Bake at 250° for 1 hour, stirring 3 or 4 times. Cool on cookie sheets before storing in tightly covered containers.

Chewy P.B. Sandwiches*

4-6 sandwiches

1 c. peanut butter
2 bananas, mashed
2 large carrots, grated

½ c. raisins
2 c. alfalfa sprouts

Combine peanut butter, bananas, carrots and raisins. Spread on whole wheat bread and top with alfalfa sprouts. This mixture turns brown if not used right away, but just stir it again and it looks and tastes fine. Great for hiking.

Anything we are supposed to have Mother Nature places at our doorstep. At twelve noon, we walk out the door and we know where Mother Nature's sun will be. Her rain comes down to us, and her air and her wind. But birds fly away when we approach and animals scamper at the sound of our footsteps. It's as though they know we can't be trusted. Apples don't run away from us. They fall off the trees into our waiting hands. Oranges, pears and peaches don't try to escape. They remain in Mother Nature's kitchen, being baked and ripened by her natural sunlight.

— Dick Gregory

Garbanzo Bean Spread*

3 cups

3 c. cooked or canned garbanzo
   beans, mashed to a paste
½ tsp. garlic powder
¼ tsp. black pepper
1 tsp. chives

2 Tbsp. prepared Dijon or other
   mustard
10 shakes hot pepper sauce
½ c. toasted sunflower seeds (optional)

Combine all ingredients and blend until smooth, either in a food processor or by hand. If using a food processor the sunflower seeds can be added either before or after processing.

This spread is equally good on crackers, raw vegetables, or in sandwiches. Try it with sweet pickle.

Guacamole*

1½ cups

2 ripe avocados
1 medium tomato, chopped
½ tsp. garlic powder
1 Tbsp. lemon juice

few drops hot pepper sauce
½ tsp. chili powder
salt to taste

Peel and mash avocados. Add remaining ingredients and mix. Serve with corn chips or use in Mexican dishes or sandwiches.

Hummus*

2 cups

½ c. sesame seeds
2 Tbsp. olive oil
3 cloves garlic, minced
¼ c. oil
1 Tbsp. parsley

1 tsp. salt
¼ c. lemon juice
1 16-oz can garbanzo beans, drained,
   liquid reserved

Blend sesame seeds in blender until powdery. Add olive oil and blend briefly. Add garlic, oil, parsley, salt and lemon juice and blend again. Add beans, blending until beans are crushed. Add bean liquid if necessary, to bring the mixture to the consistency of mashed potatoes. Chill.

Serve with vegetables (celery, carrot sticks, mushrooms, alfalfa sprouts, avocado and tomato are nice) and pocket bread cut into fourths.

Instant (Almost) Bean Dip*

About 1½ quarts

1 16-oz. can vegetarian beans in
    tomato sauce, undrained
1 16-oz. can garbanzo beans, drained
1 16-oz. can kidney beans, drained
¼ c. barbeque sauce
1 Tbsp. dried onion flakes

½ tsp. garlic powder
3 Tbsp. Italian Salad Dressing
1 tomato, chopped
1 avocado, peeled and chopped
2 green onions, chopped

Hand mash or blend beans to a thick paste. Add barbeque sauce, dried onion, garlic powder and salad dressing. Stir to blend well. Just before serving add remaining ingredients. Serve with tortilla chips.

THE GREAT STAKE OUT.

Olive-Nut Spread*

1½-2 cups

¾ c. pecan pieces
1½ c. walnut pieces
¾ c. stuffed green olives

4-6 Tbsp. tofu mayonnaise or
regular mayonnaise

Blend nuts in blender on high, blending only one handful at a time, then removing and blending the next handful. Mince green olives. Mix all ingredients well and chill.

This is an excellent cracker spread or sandwich filling. It can be made without using a blender, but the pate-like consistency achieved by using the blender is a plus. It's even better if pecans are used to replace the walnuts.

Spinach Spread*

1½-2 cups

2 10-oz. pkgs. frozen chopped
spinach, thawed, drained and
excess moisture squeezed out
½ c. sliced green onion
½ c. dried parsley

½ tsp. salt
generous amount of freshly ground
black pepper
1 c. tofu mayonnaise or
regular mayonnaise

Mix together well and chill. Serve with crackers or use as a sandwich spread.

I believe I am not interested to know whether vivisection produces results that are profitable to the human race or doesn't. To know that the results are profitable to the race would not remove my hostility to it. The pain which it inflicts upon unconsenting animals is the basis of my enmity toward it, and it is to me sufficient justification of the enmity without looking further.

— Mark Twain

Stuffed Mushroom Caps*

24 caps

24 large mushrooms
2 cloves garlic, minced
½ c. margarine
1 c. soft bread crumbs

½ c. grated cheese, any kind (optional)
½ tsp. salt
¼ tsp. pepper
2 Tbsp. parsley

Remove stems from mushrooms and chop stems finely. Saute with garlic in 3 Tbsp. margarine until soft. Add bread crumbs, cheese, salt, pepper and parsley. Fill mushroom caps, piling in the filling and rounding off with the inside of a tablespoon. Place on greased cookie sheet. Melt remaining margarine and drizzle over mushrooms.

Bake at 350° for 15 minutes.

These will still be tasty if you prefer to use less margarine. If made much ahead of serving time they turn dark but still taste good.

Tahini*

1 cup

1 c. sesame seeds
   (hulled or "as is")

¼ c. oil
½ tsp. salt

Spread seeds in cookie pan and brown for 10 minutes at 350°, stirring after 5 minutes. Place seeds in blender and blend to a powder. Add salt. With blender running, slowly add oil. Most commercial tahini is made from hulled sesame seeds, but this is just as good.

Snacks

*Cheesy-Tasting Toast**

1 serving

1 piece bread
2 Tbsp. good flaked nutritional yeast
2 tsp. margarine

Spread margarine on bread and sprinkle with yeast. Place on cookie sheet under broiler and broil just until margarine is bubbly and yeast begins to turn light brown in places. Watch closely to prevent burning. Serve immediately.

*Saltine Toppers**

Saltine crackers have that special something to make them the perfect combination with either raisins or avocados. Really! Top a cracker with a sprinkle of raisins, hold it straight so they don't fall off, and munch. Or peel and slice an avocado, use slices to top about ten saltines, and enjoy.

*Festive Popcorn**

Sprinkle freshly popped corn with soy sauce, then toss well. Sprinkle nutritional yeast over corn and toss again. The yeast will adhere to the corn better if the corn has been popped in oil or is coated with a little margarine first.

Note: An asterisk after the recipe title means the recipe is (or can be made) vegan, using no eggs or dairy products.

Soups

If you are not an expert in the kitchen, soup is a good start for your culinary adventures. Little more is necessary than a sharp knife and a big kettle. Oh yes, there is one more thing — you'll need vegetable broth or vegetable stock for most of the recipes, though water can be used to replace either.

Vegetable broth can be made using bouillon cubes, powder, or packets. Check our lists of animal ingredients in food (p. 21) for vegetarian brand names.

Vegetable stock can be made using the recipe in this chapter. If you hate to use a perfectly good carrot just to make stock, you have an option. You can save about a week's worth of well-washed trimmings from vegetables (including potatoes) used in other dishes. Nearly any vegetable will work *except* for those in the cabbage family, such as broccoli, cauliflower, and brussels sprouts — they produce a gas while cooking. Use the saved-up trimmings to replace the carrots, potatoes, and celery in our stock recipe, and follow the same cooking instructions.

Experiment with your favorite soup recipes to make them vegetarian or vegan. If a recipe starts with frying a piece of bacon or a ham-hock, substitute a couple of tablespoons of margarine and a tiny dash of liquid hickory smoke flavor, and continue the recipe from there.

Try Savory Tofu®, a baked tofu product found in health food stores, to replace chicken or turkey. And TVP granules can nicely fill in for ground beef. Keep in mind they triple in bulk when rehydrated.

In most recipes for cream soups, the milk or cream can be directly replaced with a liquid non-dairy creamer or soymilk with delicious results. See our cream soup recipes for ideas.

Most soups keep well in the refrigerator for a week (those containing cheese don't last that long). At the end of a long day when you don't feel like cooking, a big pot of vegetarian soup will be a welcome sight. And heated soup can travel to work with you in a wide-mouth thermos as a wholesome lunch-time treat.

Note: An asterisk after the recipe title means the recipe is (or can be made) vegan, using no eggs or dairy products.

Barley-Lentil Soup*

½ lb. lentils
1¼ qts. water
¾ c. barley
2 Tbsp. oil
1 medium onion, chopped
1 rib celery, chopped

1 large potato, chopped (unpeeled)
1 large carrot, diced
1 16-oz. can tomatoes, cut up
¼ tsp. salt
dash pepper

Combine all ingredients in a large kettle. Bring to a boil, reduce heat and simmer, covered, for 2 hours or until ingredients are very tender and soup is thick. Stir occasionally to prevent sticking, and add additional water or tomato juice if the soup becomes too thick.

Basic Vegetable Stock*

2½ quarts

3 large carrots
1 large potato
2 stalks celery
2 large onions, peeled
2 Tbsp. margarine
3 quarts water

2 tsp. salt
1 bay leaf
½ tsp. basil
½ tsp. thyme
¼ tsp. freshly ground pepper
¼ tsp. garlic powder

Wash but do not peel vegetables (except onions). Chop into large pieces. Heat margarine in Dutch-oven type pan. Saute all vegetables, stirring, over medium heat for about 15 minutes. Add the water and seasonings; bring to a boil. Cover, reduce heat and simmer for 1 hour or longer. Strain. Stock can be refrigerated for up to one week or frozen.

*Perhaps that intimation, that twinge, is the tugging of a spiritual gyroscope trying to guide us toward what we already know: that killing animals is a nasty business made all the worse when the slaughter is unnecessary; that many of us wear the mantle of predator lightly and uncomfortably; that **all** life is worthy of mutual consideration and compassion; and that respect for the rights of others doesn't end with the human race. Respect for a fish? Consideration for a chicken? Is this anthropomorphic vegetarian sentimentality, or can a case be made for the rights of animals? "Because the heart beats under a covering of hair, feathers, or wings, is it therefore, to be of no account?"*

— The Vegetarian Alternative

Cauliflower Cheese Soup

1½ quarts

1 large potato, cut in cubes
1 large onion, diced
2 carrots, diced
3 cloves garlic, thinly sliced
½ tsp. salt

½ tsp. salt
1 large cauliflower,
  broken into flowerettes
1 quart soy milk or milk
1 c. grated cheddar cheese

In a saucepan, barely cover the potatoes, onion, carrots, garlic and salt with water. Cover and cook over medium heat until tender. In a blender, puree this mixture in its own water. Steam the cauliflower, lightly salted, until tender. Combine the pureed vegetables, cauliflower, soymilk and cheese. Heat very slowly. Do not cook. Serve immediately when hot, topped with a little extra grated cheese if desired.

Corn Chowder*

3 Tbsp. margarine
1 medium onion, peeled and chopped
1 stalk celery, thinly sliced
1 green pepper, diced
2 small potatoes, diced
3 c. water or vegetable stock
½ tsp. turmeric (optional)
½ tsp. basil
3 c. corn (fresh or frozen)

3 Tbsp. flour
1 c. Mocha Mix® (or other non-dairy
  creamer or soymilk)
2 Tbsp. parsley, chopped
1 tsp. salt
¼ tsp. pepper, fresh ground
chopped green onion and artificial
  bacon bits for garnish

Heat margarine in a large, heavy kettle. Stir in the onion, green pepper, and celery, and saute until just tender. Add the potatoes, stock, next two seasonings, and corn. Simmer, covered, until potatoes are barely tender, about 30 minutes. Mix flour with a little of the Mocha Mix.® When well-blended, add the remainder of the Mocha Mix® and stir into the soup. Cook on low heat until thickened, about 5 minutes. Stir in salt, pepper and parlsey, ladle into bowls, and garnish.

Note: Fresh corn on the cob makes this recipe extra delicious. After cutting corn off the cob with a sharp knife, use the back of the knife to scrape the cob, extracting the corn pulp. Add this to the soup along with the Mocha Mix®.

Creamy Mushroom Soup*

6 servings

1 lb. fresh mushrooms, washed, sliced
3 Tbsp. margarine, divided
1 small onion, peeled and chopped
½ tsp. celery salt
½ tsp. basil
2 packets MBT vegetable broth
(or other brand)

3 c. boiling water
3 Tbsp. flour
1 c. Mocha Mix® (or other non-
dairy liquid creamer or soymilk)
1 tsp. salt
¼ tsp. pepper

In large saucepan, heat 2 Tbsp. of the margarine. Saute mushrooms and onions until beginning to turn tender. Meanwhile combine boiling water, the bouillon packets, 1 Tbsp. margarine, the flour, and Mocha Mix® Set aside.

Add celery salt and basil to the mushrooms and stir well. Then add the broth mixture and stir until soup thickens. Season with salt and pepper.

Note: This soup can be used to replace canned cream of mushroom soup in recipes.

Gazpacho*

1½ quarts

3 tomatoes
1½ cucumbers, peeled and cut in chunks
1½ onions, cut up
(Walla Walla Sweets if possible)
1½ c. tomato juice
1½ green peppers, cut up

½ c. olive oil
1 c. vinegar
¾ Tbsp. hot pepper sauce
3 tsp. salt
¼ tsp. pepper

In a blender, puree the tomatoes, cucumbers, onions, tomato juice and green peppers. Mix in the remaining ingredients and refrigerate a minimum of 2 hours. Serve chilled, topped with croutons, diced onions, diced cucumbers and diced green peppers.

Those who still eat flesh when they could do otherwise have no claim to be serious moralists.
— Stephen R. L. Clark
from **The Moral Status of Animals**

Grandpa's Tomato Soup*

4 servings

3 medium tomatoes, chopped fine
(or 1 16-oz. can stewed tomatoes)
½ medium onion, chopped fine
1 stalk celery, chopped fine
4 Tbsp. margarine, divided
2 tsp. sugar
3 Tbsp. flour

2 16-oz. cans tomato juice
1 tsp. salt
¼ tsp. freshly ground black pepper
½ tsp. basil
¼ tsp. thyme
¼ tsp. garlic

Melt 2 Tbsp. of the margarine in a large saucepan over medium heat. Add tomatoes, onion, celery, and sugar. Break up tomato chunks as they cook.

When onion is tender, add tomato juice and seasonings. As soup begins to boil, ladle out one cup of the hot liquid and combine with other 2 Tbsp. of margarine and the flour. Return to the pot. Reduce heat to low and cook another 5 minutes to thicken.

Note: This soup may be used to replace canned tomato soup called for in recipes.

Creamy Tomato Soup*

4 servings

Follow directions for **Grandpa's Tomato Soup**, using half the required amount of tomato juice. Ladle out one cup of the hot soup and combine with margarine and flour as previously directed; then add 2 cups Mocha Mix.® Stir well, return to hot soup and simmer just until thickened.

Northern Delight*

1-1½ quarts

4 Tbsp. oil
1 small onion, diced
½ c. sliced mushrooms
1 heaping tsp. curry powder
1½ c. brown rice
5 c. water

¾ c. split peas
2 small potatoes, cut into chunks and
steamed until barely tender
2 large carrots, diced and lightly
steamed
salt

Saute onions in oil until tender. Add mushrooms, saute a few minutes, and add curry powder. Add rice and continue to saute for several minutes.

Pour in water. bring to a boil, then cook an additional 20 to 30 minutes. Add peas. Let mixture boil down. When peas are soft and soup is desired consistency, add potatoes and carrots and season with salt. Heat through and serve.

Pepper Pot Soup*

6 to 8 servings

½ c. Granburger® or other TVP,
    soaked in ½ c. water
½ c. minced onion
1 c. diced green pepper
½ c. diced celery
2 Tbsp. margarine
2 qts. boiling water
4 cubes vegetable bouillon or
    4 tsp. bouillon powder

10 crushed peppercorns
1 bay leaf
1 tsp. thyme
½ c. diced carrots
½ c. diced potatoes
1 c. canned or fresh tomatoes,
    in chunks
1 tsp. salt
½ tsp. marjoram

In a large kettle, saute the TVP, onion, green pepper and celery in margarine until crisp-tender. Add water and bouillon cubes. Tie up the peppercorns, bay leaf and thyme in cheesecloth and add. Cover, simmer 45 minutes. Add the carrots and potatoes and simmer for an additional 30 minutes. Remove cheesecloth bundle and add remaining ingredients. Cook 5-10 minutes more. Serve with freshly ground pepper and imitation bacon bits, if desired.

Split Pea Soup*

About 1½ quarts

2 c. split peas
8 c. cold water
2/3 c. imitation bacon bits (optional)
1 clove garlic

1 large onion, chopped
1 stalk celery, whole
2 carrots, chopped
salt and pepper

Combine ingredients in a large soup pan. Bring to a boil and simmer until the peas become soft (2-3 hours). Remove the celery stalk and serve.

A vegetarian diet can prevent 90% of our thromboemboli (strokes) and 97% of our coronary occlusions (heart attacks).

— Editorial
Journal of the American Medical Assoc.
June 3, 1961

Spinach Lentil Soup with Marinated Rice*

5 to 6 servings

3 c. hot cooked rice
½ c. oil
½ c. vinegar
2 tsp. basil
¼ c. chopped green onion
6 c. water
1½ c. lentils

1/3 c. olive oil
2 large onions, sliced
3 cloves garlic, minced
1½ tsp. coriander
½ tsp. salt
1½ lb. spinach, sliced
¼ c. lemon juice or vinegar

To the hot rice add the ½ c. oil, ½ c. vinegar, basil and green onions. Cover and chill at least 2 hours.

Meanwhile, bring water and lentils to a boil in a large pot. Cover and simmer over low heat until lentils are tender (about 40 minutes). In a frying pan combine olive oil, onion and garlic. Cook over medium-high heat, stirring, until onion is limp and golden (about 20 minutes). Add coriander and salt. Add the onion mixture to the cooked lentils, stir, and add the spinach. Simmer, uncovered, for 10 minutes. Add the lemon juice. To serve, spoon the marinated rice into individual bowls of lentil soup.

Summer Vegetable Soup*

6 servings

3 Tbsp. margarine
1 medium onion, peeled and chopped
1 stalk celery, sliced thinly
1 large carrot, sliced thinly
2 small potatoes, diced
2 large tomatoes, diced
4 c. vegetable stock

5 fresh basil leaves, torn into
    tiny pieces (or 1 tsp. dry basil)
2 small zucchini, sliced ¼" thick
1 lb. green beans, cut into 2" pieces
1 tsp. salt
¼ tsp. pepper

In a Dutch-oven type pan, heat margarine. Add onion, celery, and carrot. Cook, stirring, over medium heat for about 10 minutes. Add potatoes, tomatoes, stock, and basil. Cover and bring to a boil. Reduce heat and simmer for 15 minutes. Add zucchini, green beans and simmer for another 15 minutes. Season with salt and pepper.

Swiss Potato Soup*

1½ quarts

1½ quarts water
4 cubes vegetable bouillon or
    4 tsp. bouillon powder
2 large onions, sliced
2 large potatoes, diced
    (peeled or unpeeled)
2 c. celery, sliced

8 mushrooms, sliced
1/3 c. margarine
1/3 c. flour
1 c. grated Swiss cheese for garnish
    (optional)
2-3 Tbsp. chopped parsley for garnish

In a large kettle combine water, bouillon, onions, potatoes, celery and mushrooms. Cover and simmer 30 minutes or until potatoes are just tender. In a saucepan, melt margarine over medium-low heat and slowly add flour, stirring constantly until golden brown. Add this sauce to the soup mixture. Cook over medium heat until the soup thickens and bubbles. Add salt and pepper to taste. Serve with parsley and grated Swiss cheese, if desired.

The average meat- and fish-eating American, during his/her lifetime, is personally responsible for the needless suffering in "factory farms" and for the slaughter of 50 cows, calves, pigs, and sheep, more than 1,000 chickens and turkeys, as well as uncounted thousands of fish.

— Veg. Information Service

Side Dishes

We have included some pretty hearty recipes here. You'll find that one of these concoctions plus a salad and some soup and/or bread will be a very filling meal.

The stuffing recipes are presented in hopes that this Thanksgiving will bring peace to you and your favorite turkey.

Baked Beans*

6-8 servings

1 lb. pinto or great northern beans
1 large onion, chopped
2 tsp. salt
1 8-oz. can tomato sauce

½-1/3 c. sweetener (brown sugar, honey, molasses or a combination)
½ tsp. ginger
2 tsp. prepared mustard
dash hot pepper sauce

Soak beans overnight.

In a large pot, cover beans with water to 1 inch above beans. Simmer for 2-3 hours until soft, adding water if needed. Drain and reserve broth. Add all remaining ingredients, plus 1 c. of the bean broth, to the beans in a casserole or bean crock. Cover.

Bake at 350° for 2-3 hours.

The risk factor for heart disease is approximately three time higher for meat eaters than vegetarians. For colon cancer it is approximately twice as high and it is three times higher in the case of breast cancer.
— Veg. Information Service

Note: An asterisk after the recipe title means the recipe is (or can be made) vegan, using no eggs or dairy products.

Bread Dressing*

6 servings

¼ c. margarine
¼ c. parsley
1 tsp. basil
¾ tsp. salt
⅛ tsp. nutmeg
½ tsp. paprika
½ tsp. garlic powder
2 tsp. coriander
2 tsp. rosemary

1 c. tofu, drained and crumbled (½ lb.)
1 c. chopped celery
1 carrot, diced
1 parsnip, diced
½ c. walnut pieces
½ c. raisins
1 8-oz. can crushed pineapple, drained,
   liquid reserved
1 loaf day-old bread, cubed

In a large frying pan melt the margarine over medium-high heat. Add parsley, basil, salt, nutmeg, paprika, garlic powder, coriander and rosemary. Add the tofu and cook until the tofu is light brown. Add the celery, carrot and parsnip. Continue cooking until vegetables are tender. Combine vegetable mixture with bread. Add walnuts, raisins and pineapple. Moisten with pineapple liquid or vegetable stock.

Bake at 350° for 1 hour in a covered pan.

Bulgur Pilaf*

4 servings

2 Tbsp. margarine
½ c. chopped celery
1 medium onion, chopped
1 c. bulgur, uncooked
¼ tsp. dill weed
¼ tsp. oregano

½ tsp. salt
¼ tsp. pepper
2 c. water or vegetable broth
½ c. sliced mushrooms
1 Tbsp. chopped parsley
2 Tbsp. chopped pimiento

Melt margarine in a large skillet. Add celery, onion and bulgur. Stir constantly over medium-high heat until vegetables are golden and bulgur is golden. Add seasonings and water. Cover and bring to a boil. Reduce heat and simmer 10 minutes, covered. Add mushrooms and simmer 5 minutes more, covered. Stir in parsley and pimiento just before serving.

Chopped green pepper, chopped nuts, grated carrots or sliced ripe olives make nice additions to this dish.

Grilled Tomatoes*

6 servings

3 large tomatoes
3 green onions, chopped
1 c. chopped mushrooms

juice of ½ lemon
2 Tbsp. oil
salt to taste

Cut tomatoes in half and make 3 or 4 cuts through the pulp of each half. Arrange on baking sheet, cut sides up. Pile tops with chopped onion and mushroom. Squeeze lemon juice and sprinkle oil over tops. Bake at 350-400 degrees for 20 to 30 minutes, or until mushrooms look crisp.

Irish Potatoes and Cabbage*

4 servings

1 c. water
3 large potatoes, peeled and diced
½ head green cabbage, shredded
tops of 1 bunch green onions, chopped

¾ c. Mocha Mix® liquid creamer
pinch of mace
salt and pepper to taste
1-2 Tbsp. margarine

Boil the potatoes in 1 c. water until nearly tender. Add cabbage and boil 5 minutes more. Drain. Add green onion tops and creamer. Beat until smooth. Add seasonings. Dot top with margarine and garnish with a few reserved green onion tops.

Nancy's Rice*

6 servings

4 Tbsp. tamari or soy sauce
½ c. raw cashews
2 c. brown rice
2 medium onions, chopped

1 c. chopped mushrooms
½ c. chopped celery
¼ c. melted margarine

Prepare cashews by sprinkling them with 1 Tbsp. of the tamari and baking at 200° for 2 hours.

Cook rice according to package directions, adding 1 of the chopped onions and 3 Tbsp. tamari to the rice-water mixture before cooking. Saute remaining onion, mushrooms and celery in margarine until tender. Add to cooked rice. Stir in cashews, sprinkling a few on top as garnish.

Potatoes and Gravy*

4 servings

4 medium potatoes, scrubbed and
  quartered (peeled if desired)
1½ c. water
2 Tbsp. margarine
2 Tbsp. whole wheat flour

1½ Tbsp. nutritional yeast
2 tsp. soy sauce
pepper to taste
½ c. sliced mushrooms and/or
  ½ c. sliced onions (optional)

Boil potatoes in water in a covered saucepan until tender, about 10 minutes. Reserve cooking liquid. In a large skillet, melt margarine over medium heat. If using mushrooms or onions, saute until soft and proceed with remaining steps. To melted margarine, stir in flour and yeast, using a whisk. The mixture will be quite dry. Over medium heat, stir in cooking liquid from potatoes, whisking until smooth. Season with soy sauce and pepper. Add the potatoes and heat through.

Raisin-Apple Dressing*

6 servings

1 loaf day-old bread
1 c. raisins
1 c. boiling water
1 cube vegetable bouillon, or
  1 tsp. powder bouillon
3 Tbsp. oil
1 onion, diced

1 c. diced celery
2 apples, diced
¼ c. finely chopped parsley
1 tsp. garlic powder
1 tsp. onion salt
1 tsp. salt
1 tsp. sage

The night before preparing, cut bread into ½-inch cubes and spread on a cookie sheet to dry.

Combine raisins and dry bread in a bowl. Dissolve bouillon in the water. Over medium-high heat, saute the onion and celery in oil for 3 minutes in a skillet. Combine with the bread mixture, then add apples, parsley, garlic powder, onion salt, salt and sage. Add the bouillon mixture and stir well. Cover.

Bake at 350° for 30 minutes.

It is so surprising to hear people speak of cruelty to animals and wishing that it could be immediately abolished, while each day they themselves are contributing to this cruelty by eating the flesh of animals.

— *Shrimati Rukmini Devi Arundale*
former member of the Parliament of India

Refried Beans*

2 cups

1 c. dry pinto beans
2-3 Tbsp. oil
pinch oregano
2-3 cloves garlic or 1 tsp. garlic powder

1 tsp. salt
1/3 c. oil
¼ c. finely chopped onion

Soak beans overnight.

In a large pot, cover beans with water 1 inch above beans. Add 2-3 Tbsp. oil, oregano, garlic and salt. Simmer for 2-5 hours (about 3 hours usually works well). Add hot water if needed.

In a hot frying pan or skillet, heat the 1/3 c. oil and add the onion. Add the cooked beans and juice 1 c. at a time, mashing coarsely until all beans are added. When the mixture begins to dry, it will start to come away from the edge of the pan. While cooking, tilt the pan from side to side until the beans form a loose roll (15-20 minutes). Tip roll onto a plate.

For variation, add ½ tsp. cumin or 1 tsp. hot pepper sauce.

Savory Rice*

4-6 servings

½ c. margarine
1 1/3 c. rice
1 c. chopped celery
¼ c. chopped onion
¼ c. chopped celery leaves

1½ tsp. salt
pinch each: black pepper, sage, thyme
¼ tsp. marjoram
1 1/3 c. water

Over medium-high heat melt the margarine in a large skillet. Add remaining ingredients, except water, and saute 8 minutes. Add the water, bring to a boil quickly, cover and remove from heat.

Bake in a preheated 375° oven for 15 minutes.

Steamed Vegetables with Herbed Olive Oil*

4-6 servings

1 summer squash, sliced
2 c. cauliflowerettes
2 c. broccoli flowers and thinly
  sliced stems
2 c. Chinese pea pods (or 1 10-oz.
  pkg. frozen, thawed)

2 c. sliced mushrooms
1 carrot, thinly sliced
1 Tbsp. Fines Herb (or your favorite
  herb blend or seasoning salt)
¼ c. cold-pressed olive oil

Steam all vegetables just until tender. Before serving, sprinkle top with olive oil mixed with Fines Herbs.

Stir-Fried Yams*

4-6 servings

2 c. thinly-sliced skinned yams
¼ c. oil, or more as needed
2 or 3 medium yellow onions,
  sliced

1 c. chopped celery
2 c. broccoli flowers and thinly-sliced
  stems
2 c. sliced mushrooms
¼ c. raw sesame seeds

Fry yams in oil over medium-high heat until tender. Add onion, broccoli and mushrooms and continue frying until all are tender. Add sesame seeds and fry mixture for 3 minutes more.

My situation is a solemn one. Life is offered to me on the condition of eating beefsteaks. But death is better than cannibalism. My will contains directions for my funeral, which will be followed not my mourning coaches, but by oxen, sheep, flocks of poultry, and a small traveling aquarium of live fish, all wearing white scarves in honor of the man who perished rather than eat his fellow creatures. It will be, with the exception of Noah's Ark, the most remarkable thing of its kind ever seen.

— George Bernard Shaw
upon being told by doctors that he
would die if he refused to eat meat

Stir-Fry Vegetables*

4 servings

1 c. thinly sliced carrots
½ c. chopped green onions
2 c. small cauliflowerettes
1 10-oz. pkg. frozen Italian green
   beans, thawed and drained

¼ lb. mushrooms, sliced
¼ c. oil
1 Tbsp. lemon juice
1 Tbsp. summer savory

Fry all vegetables in oil in large skillet for 3 to 5 minutes, adding lemon juice and sprinkling in savory near end.

Unstuffed Stuffing

6 servings

3 Tbsp. margarine
1 c. chopped celery
1 c. chopped onion
1 16-oz. box dried stuffing

1 egg
½ c. wheat germ
1 8-oz. bag cranberries, sorted
   and washed

Saute celery and onions in margarine until tender. Add remaining ingredients and mix.

Bake at 400° in a covered dish for 40 minutes.

Vegetable and Cashew "Quiche"*

4 servings

½ c. raw cashews
1 stalk celery, diced
1 carrot, diced
1 onion, diced

3 Tbsp. oil
½ c. water
2 Tbsp. cornstarch
1 Tbsp. warm water

Broil raw cashews until golden brown. Stir-fry vegetables in hot oil until tender-crisp, about 2 minutes. Add ½ c. water and bring to a boil. In a small bowl mix cornstarch with 1 Tbsp. warm water. Add to boiling vegetables and continue to cook until the mixture reaches the desired consistency. Pour into a serving bowl and top with cashews.

Sauces and Gravies

One reason traditional American meals remain popular is because they are "hearty." Hearty. It is indefinable, but somehow a hearty meal fills up all the corners and cravings we feel when we sit down for a family-type meal. Of course, there are countless vegetarian meals which make the grade, but if you are in your usual hurry or in an occasional quandary over what to prepare, sauces and gravies can often answer your needs. Sauces are versatile if they are anything. Adding a gravy or a sauce to your usual meal can make it fancier, more interesting, and definitely hearty.

The sauces and gravies in this section are made without any eggs or dairy products. Some of the gravies, through spices alone, taste amazingly similar to homestyle traditional gravies made with drippings from you-know-what.

*Barbeque Sauce**

2½ cups

1 15-oz. can tomato sauce	1 tsp. lemon juice
½ c. vinegar	1 tsp. prepared mustard
1 tsp. garlic powder	dash hot pepper sauce
½ tsp. liquid smoke	1 Tbsp. soy sauce or tamari
¼ c. molasses or brown sugar	2-4 Tbsp. minced onion (optional)

Combine all ingredients in a small saucepan and cook over medium heat until simmering.

Barbeque — with no meat? Try this sauce with beans or use it to baste a shish-kabob of eggplant, peppers, potatoes and onions. It adds zip to any kind of potatoes, and is delicious when used to baste well-fried tofu slices.

Note: An asterisk after the recipe title means the recipe is (or can be made) vegan, using no eggs or dairy products.

Brown Gravy*

2½-3 cups

½ c. whole wheat or white flour
¼ c. oil or margarine
2 c. water
½ tsp. black pepper
¾ tsp. garlic powder

1 tsp. cumin
2 tsp. coriander
½ tsp. chili powder
3 Tbsp. soy sauce or tamari

Place flour in a clean, unoiled skillet and let it brown for a few minutes over medium-high heat, stirring to avoid burning. Turn heat to low and mix in oil. Slowly add water, stirring constantly with a whisk to avoid lumping. Add spices and soy sauce and simmer until thick.

For variety, add ½ c. thinly sliced mushrooms or ¼ c. minced onion after adding the oil. Cook until soft before adding water and continuing with the remaining steps.

Brown gravy is good with noodles, potatoes, rice and other grains. It's an excellent addition to open-face sandwiches or used in stews or hearty vegetable pies.

The silent cry of millions of creatures should be louder in our ears than all the din of the world. Will those who have ears to hear, answer their call and redeem our country from the superstitution that animals are created for man and his pleasure alone?

— Shrimati Rukmini Devi Arundale
former member of the Parliament of India

Cashew Gravy*

1½ cups

1 Tbsp. margarine
1 Tbsp. flour
1 packet MBT vegetable broth mix
(or other brand)

1 c. boiling water
¼ c. cashews, browned under broiler
¼ tsp. salt
⅛ tsp. pepper

In a skillet, melt margarine over medium heat and stir in flour with a whisk. Put the water, cashews, and broth mix in blender and blend well. Pour slowly into the skillet and stir with whisk until smooth. Add salt and pepper. This is a real taste treat served over vegie-burgers or nut loaf. Or fry a piece of Savory Tofu® (available in the refrigerator section of natural food stores) and top with cashew gravy.

Chunky Spaghetti Sauce*

About 1 quart

3 or 4 small zucchini, in ¼-inch slices
1 small yellow squash, in ¼-inch slices
½ medium onion, chopped
½ green pepper, chopped
2 tomatoes, chopped
1 c. chopped mushrooms
1 15-oz. can tomato sauce

1/3 c. olive oil
½-1 tsp. salt
2 tsp. oregano
1½ tsp. garlic powder
one vegetable bouillon cube
(optional)

Mix all ingredients in a skillet or large saucepan and simmer over medium heat, stirring occasionally, until vegetables are cooked.

Holiday Gravy*

4 cups

¾ c. garbanzo flour
½ c. oil
3½ c. water
2 Tbsp. nutritional yeast
½ tsp. celery seed
¼ tsp. sage
¼ tsp. thyme
½ tsp. cumin

½ tsp. coriander
¼ tsp. garlic powder
¼ tsp. tarragon
¼ tsp. rosemary
¼ tsp. turmeric
1½ Tbsp. soy sauce or tamari
½-1 tsp. salt
2 Tbsp. lemon juice

First: if you don't have all of these spices, you can still make a good gravy by using any 2/3 of them. Don't be afraid to experiment.

In a skillet, over low heat, mix flour and oil. Slowly add the water, stirring constantly, until smooth and free of lumps. Add nutritional yeast, spices and soy sauce. Stir. Barely bring to a boil, and simmer for one minute. Remove from heat and stir in lemon juice.

This gravy can be used like a turkey or chicken gravy. It's great over potatoes, noodles, grains and stuffing. Also try it over vegetables and on hot sandwiches.

Now we don't eat anything that has to be killed for us. We've been through a lot, coming thru the '60's with all those drugs and friends dropping like flies. And we've reached the stage where we really value life.

— *Paul McCartney*

Mexican Sauce*

1½ cups

1 6-oz. can tomato paste plus ¾ c. water,
   or 1 15-oz. can tomato sauce
1 tsp. chili powder
1 tsp garlic powder or 2 cloves
   minced garlic

½ tsp. oregano
1 tsp. cumin powder
½-1 tsp. salt

Combine all ingredients in a small saucepan and simmer over medium-low heat for ½ hour.

This sauce can be varied by first sauteeing ½ medium onion, minced, in 2 Tbsp. oil before adding the other ingredients; or by adding chopped black olives before simmering.

This is a good base for burritos, enchiladas or tacos; or serve over rice, beans or cornbread.

Nutritional Yeast Sauce*

2 cups

3 Tbsp. margarine
2 Tbsp. flour
4 Tbsp. nutritional yeast
½ tsp. garlic powder or 1 clove garlic, minced
1 tsp. buttery flavored popcorn popping oil (optional)
¼ tsp. freshly ground black pepper
½ tsp. salt
1 c. boiling water
1 c. liquid non-dairy creamer or soymilk

In skillet over medium heat, melt margarine. Using a whisk, stir in flour, nutritional yeast, garlic, popcorn oil, salt and pepper. Cook, stirring, until mixture turns dry and crumbly. Slowly whisk in the boiling water, then slowly whisk in the liquid creamer. Stir until smooth.

Try this flavorful sauce on vegetables instead of cheese sauce. You can make a quick pasta dish by boiling the pasta, steaming some carrots, broccoli, and cauliflower, and mixing the pasta and vegies with the sauce. Top with sauteed mushrooms for a real treat! Other yummy combos using nutritional yeast sauce:

Pasta-garbanzo beans-peas-onions-mushrooms
Rice-celery-carrots-fried tofu-onions
Green peppers-zucchini-mushrooms-scallions-serve over baked potatoes

Onion Gravy*

2 cups

2 Tbsp. margarine
2 Tbsp. flour

1 packet onion soup mix
2 c. boiling water

Dissolve onion soup mix in the water. In skillet on medium heat, melt the margarine. Whisk in flour and cook, stirring, until mixture bubbles and turns golden. Slowly add hot onion soup, whisking, until all has been added and gravy is smooth.

This gravy is a terrific addition to mashed potatoes, a soy or vegie-burger, or a nut loaf. Sauteed mushrooms can be added to the cooked gravy.

Peanut Sauce*

2 cups

3 Tbsp. chunky peanut butter
2 Tbsp. oil
2 Tbsp. brown sugar
3 Tbsp. chili powder

3 Tbsp. soy sauce or tamari
1 c. water
2 Tbsp. lemon juice or vinegar

In a small bowl, mix peanut butter, oil, brown sugar, chili powder and soy sauce. Add water and stir. Add lemon juice and mix well. Serve at room temperature.

Peanut sauce is found in many southeast Asian dishes. Traditionally used on rice, noodles and vegetables, it's also good as a sauce over vegetable fried rice. For variety, try adding 2 Tbsp. hoisin sauce.

Quick Italian Catch-All Sauce*

2 cups

1 15-oz. can tomato sauce
2 tsp. oregano
1 tsp. garlic powder or 2-3 cloves
   minced garlic

1 tsp. basil
½ tsp. rosemary
salt to taste

Mix all ingredients and use as is, or add 2 Tbsp. oil (olive oil is wonderful) and simmer over medium heat until thick.

For variety, add sliced sauteed mushrooms or chopped onions, black olives or sesame seeds.

This sauce makes great spaghetti, lasagna, macaroni or pizza. It's also good simmered with zucchini and onions or mixed with fried potatoes and onions. Try it chilled as a zesty salad dressing.

Salsa*

3 cups

6 medium tomatoes, peeled and finely chopped
½ c. thinly sliced or diced canned California green chiles, seed and pith removed,
    or fresh chiles
1/3 c. minced onion
1 tsp. salt (this is necessary)
minced canned jalapeno chiles

Mix all ingredients together. About 1 jalapeno to each cup of sauce will make it noticeably hot. Serve with tortilla chips or use as a topping for Mexican dishes.

Smooth Breakfast Gravy*

2½ cups

2 c. soy milk or liquid non-dairy creamer
½ c. white flour (whole wheat will work,
    but it won't be as creamy)
1/3 c. oil

½-1 tsp. salt
⅛ tsp. pepper
1-2 Tbsp. artificial bacon bits
    (optional)

Using a whisk or fork, mix all ingredients except artificial bacon bits in a bowl. If using the artificial bacon bits, heat 2 Tbsp. oil in a skillet, add the bits and cook over medium heat just until brown — usually less than a minute, so watch carefully. Pour gravy mixture into skillet and simmer, stirring frequently to keep the gravy smooth, until it thickens.

This gravy is perfect with a country breakfast of biscuits or hashbrowns. It's also excellent for "creamed" vegetables and over crepes.

Man is destined to a better occupation than that of pursuing and cutting the throats of dumb animals.

— *Cicero*
Nothing Cruel is Useful or Expedient

Sweet and Sour Sauce*

1½ cups

1 c. water
1½ Tbsp. cornstarch
½ c. brown sugar; or, syrup from one
   13½-oz. can of pineapple chunks
   (use the pineapple in your vegetables)

2 Tbsp. oil
¼ c. vinegar
¼ c. soy sauce
1 tsp. salt
¾ tsp. chili powder

Mix cornstarch and water. Add other ingredients, pour into a sauce pan and bring to a boil over medium heat. Reduce heat and simmer for 5 minutes.

Add pineapple chunks plus stir-fried bean sprouts, green peppers and onions to the sauce and serve with rice. This sauce goes well with many vegetables or rice dishes. For an unusual taste pour it over leaf lettuce or hot potato chunks, or chill and serve as a salad dressing.

Tahini Sauce*

1¼ cups

½ c. tahini
1-2 cloves garlic, minced
1 tsp. salt

¼ c. lemon juice
½-¾ c. water

Mix all ingredients, in a blender or by hand, until smooth and of pouring consistency.

Use tahini sauce in pita (pocket) bread with falafel, or with chilled, raw vegetables.

Tartar Sauce*

1¼ cups

1 c. tofu mayonnaise or regular mayonnaise
2 Tbsp. chopped dill pickle or pickle relish
1 Tbsp. minced onion

2 tsp. chopped pimiento
1½ tsp. lemon juice
1 tsp. soy sauce

Mix all ingredients and refrigerate. Serve cold.

Tartar sauce is delicious on baked potatoes or any crispy fried foods.

"MARY HAD A LITTLE LAMB, ITS FLEECE WAS WHITE AS SNOW... "

"MARY — EAT YOUR LAMB ! "

Main Dishes

First, let us warn you — main dish, side dish, and "what vegetable shall we have" isn't really the way to think of a vegetarian dinner. With a meat-eater's diet, everything revolves around what kind of meat you choose, while the extras play second-best. To allow yourself the greatest choice, you have got to quit thinking like that, because you aren't, in most cases, going to directly substitute one vegetarian item for that piece of meat that you always before planned your menu around. A vegetarian meal often consists of one dish with everything mixed in, or two items, the decision of which is more "main" than the other being difficult. The traditional labels, then, don't mean a thing. So, in this section, we've tried our best to select good, hearty entrees — but please also look into "salads" and "sides," as there, too, you might find a variety of combinations that will satisfy your mealtime needs.

*Brown Rice Stir Fry**

3-4 servings

3 c. cooked brown rice (1½ c. raw)
2 Tbsp. oil
1 quarter-sized slice fresh ginger root
3 tsp. minced garlic
½ c. slivered blanched almonds

2 large or 3 small bunches green onions
5 ribs celery, sliced diagonally in
 ¼-inch pieces
3 Tbsp. soy sauce or tamari

Heat oil in wok or large frying pan to 375° (high). Add the ginger root, garlic and almonds and cook, stirring constantly, just until almonds begin to turn golden, about 3 minutes. Add onions and continue cooking 2-3 minutes more. Remove ginger slice. Add celery and cook another 4 minutes, stirring, until celery just begins to become tender-crisp. Add the cooked rice and soy sauce. Stir until the rice is heated through and serve immediately. This is best when the vegetables have a definite crispness; don't let it get mushy.

Note: An asterisk after the recipe title means the recipe is (or can be made) vegan, using no eggs or dairy products.

Chanterelle/Champion

2 servings

2 c. large mushrooms, chanterelles
   if possible
2 Tbsp. butter or margarine
½ c. dry white wine or sherry

½ c. seedless green grapes
¼ c. whipping or heavy cream
3 c. cooked pilaf, barley or noodles

Saute mushrooms in butter. Combine wine, grapes and cream, and simmer 5 minutes over low heat. Add mushrooms. Serve over pilaf, barley or noodles.

Creamy Spinach-Mushroom Squares*

4-6 servings

2 large onions, chopped
¾ lb. mushrooms, sliced (about 3 c.)
3 Tbsp. margarine
1 lb. soft tofu, or 1 lb. firm tofu plus 2 Tbsp. water or vegetable broth
3 tsp. vegetable bouillon powder, or 3 cubes bouillon, crushed
2 10-oz. pkgs. frozen chopped spinach, thawed and very well drained
½ tsp. basil
¼ tsp. nutmeg
1/3 c. dried breadcrumbs or crushed crackers
salt and pepper for seasoning

In a large skillet, saute onions and mushrooms in margarine over medium-high heat for 10-15 minutes, until soft. Remove from heat. Blend tofu in blender until smooth. Add bouillon powder and blend again. Combine all ingredients and stir to mix well. Spread in a 9-inch square greased pan.

Bake, uncovered, at 350° for 45-50 minutes. Cut into squares to serve.

For variety, saute ¼ c. dried bread crumbs in 2 Tbsp. margarine and sprinkle over the top before baking.

Those who comment over the barbarism that comes out of barbarism are like people who wish to eat their meat without slaughtering the calf. They are willing to eat the calf, but they dislike the sight of blood. They are easily satisfied if the butcher washes his hands before weighing the meat.

      — *Bertolt Brecht*
      from ***Writing the Truth: Five Difficulties***

Eggplant Burger*

8-12 servings

1 large eggplant, peeled and sliced in ½-inch thick discs, and then soaked in
  well-salted water for 15-20 minutes if time permits
½ c. whole wheat or garbanzo flour
1 Tbsp. oil, or more, for frying
1 Tbsp. soy sauce

Dip eggplant slices in flour to coat them. If the flour will not adhere, moisten the slices with a little water or oil first. In a skillet, fry the slices over medium heat in a combination of oil and soy sauce, until tender in the center. Serve on bread with mustard, catsup, onion slices and relish.

Eggplant Medley*

4 servings

1 c. dry rice or couscous, cooked
  according to package directions
2 Tbsp. vegetable oil
1 large eggplant, peeled and cubed
1 large onion, chopped
2 summer squash, sliced ¼" thick
2 cloves garlic, minced

1 tsp. oregano
1 tsp. salt
¼ tsp. pepper
1 can tomato juice (16 oz.)
2 tomatoes, diced
1 c. cashews, broiled in oven until
  brown

In Dutch-oven type pan, heat oil. Saute onion, garlic, squash, and eggplant, until barely tender. Add seasonings and turn heat to low. Add rice or couscous, tomatoes, and tomato juice. Simmer ½ hour. Top with the browned cashews just before serving.

Ellie's Millet, Barley, Brown Rice Combo

4 servings

4 c. water
4 tsp. powdered vegetable bouillon,
  or 4 cubes bouillon
1 c. millet
½ c. barley

½ c. brown rice
4 c. chopped vegetables
2 c. grated white or yellow cheese
2 Tbsp. sesame seeds, optional

In a large pot, combine water and bouillon and bring to a boil. Add the grains and return to a boil. Simmer on low for 45 minutes. Cover and let stand 15 minutes.

Steam vegetables until tender-crisp. Place cooked grains in an oiled casserole and top with vegetables. Cover with cheese. Sprinkle with sesame seeds if desired.

Bake at 350°, uncovered, for 20 minutes.

Enchiladas*

12 enchiladas

½ c. oil
1 c. chopped onion
2 cloves garlic, crushed
1½ tsp. salt
6 c. cubed eggplant, in ½-inch cubes
   (2 small eggplants)
1 c. chopped green pepper

1 c. chopped toasted almonds
generous amount black pepper
1 c. crumbled and drained tofu (½ lb.)
oil for frying
12 corn tortillas
tomato sauce or hot sauce

Saute onions and garlic in oil in a large skillet over medium-high heat for 2 minutes. Add salt and cook, stirring constantly, for about 5 minutes. Stir in the eggplant. Cover, and continue cooking for about 10 minutes or until eggplant is soft. Add peppers, almonds and black pepper. Cook another 5 minutes, stirring frequently. Remove from heat and add tofu.

Heat about ½-inch of oil in a heavy skillet. Fry each tortilla on both sides, only 10 seconds per side; not enough to make them crispy. Drain on paper towels. Place about ¼ c. filling on each tortilla and roll it up. Pour tomato sauce or hot sauce over top and bake at 350° just until heated through.

Fettucine Christina

2-4 servings

1 16-oz. pkg. fettucine noodles, cooked,
   rinsed and drained (still hot)
4-6 Tbsp. butter or margarine
1 c. sliced mushrooms
1 medium onion, chopped
½ c. chopped black olives
¾ tsp. garlic powder or 2 cloves
   garlic, minced

¼ c. slivered almonds
1 8-oz. container sour half-and-half
   or sour cream
½ c. milk
½-¾ c. grated cheese
salt and pepper to taste

Saute mushrooms, onion, olives and garlic in butter until mushrooms and onion are tender. Add almonds and saute for a minute more. Combine this mixture with the cooked fettucine and add the sour cream, milk and cheese. Heat, covered, over low heat for 10 minutes, to melt the cheese and mingle the flavors.

Freshman Chole*

4 servings

2 medium onions, chopped
3 Tbsp. margarine
1 tsp. cumin seeds
1 tsp. ground cumin
1½ tsp. curry powder

2 cans garbanzo beans, drained,
   or 4 c. cooked
2 cans condensed tomato soup, or
   2 15-oz. cans tomato sauce
4-6 c. hot cooked rice

In a large frying pan, saute the onions, cumin seeds, ground cumin and curry powder in margarine over medium-high heat until the onions are just beginning to brown and tender. Add the beans and tomato soup or sauce, and cook, stirring frequently, until hot. Serve over hot rice.

I'd Rather Loaf*

4 servings

3 c. water
1½ c. lentils
2 tsp. vinegar
2 c. finely chopped walnuts
2 tsp. onion salt
½ c. bread crumbs
½ tsp. basil

½ tsp. sage
½ tsp. celery salt
1 Tbsp. soy sauce
¼ tsp. freshly ground black pepper
¼ tsp. garlic powder
4 Tbsp. melted margarine

Rinse lentils. Combine with the water and vinegar in a medium saucepan and bring to a boil. Reduce heat and cover; simmer for 30 minutes.

Drain off any excess water and mash lentils together with all other ingredients. Pour into a greased 9"x5" loaf pan and bake at 350° for one hour.

Macaroni and Chili*

4-6 servings

2 15-oz. cans kidney beans, undrained
2 ribs celery, sliced in ¼-inch pieces
1 large onion, chopped
3 cloves garlic, minced
1 15-oz. can tomatoes, cut up
1 tsp. salt
2 tsp. chili powder

½ tsp. cumin
¼ tsp. black pepper
3 Tbsp. oil
3 c. tomato juice or V-8 juice
1 c. dry elbow macaroni
2 c. shredded iceberg lettuce
½ c. chopped onion for garnish

Combine the first 11 ingredients in a large kettle. Bring to a boil over medium-high heat, reduce heat and simmer for 30 minutes. Add macaroni and simmer an additional 30 minutes, or until the macaroni is tender, adding more water or tomato juice if the mixture becomes too thick. Taste and adjust seasonings. Serve in bowls, topped with shredded lettuce and chopped onions.

Macaroni Cheese and Tomato Casserole

4 servings

1 12-oz. or 1-lb. pkg. macaroni
  (large elbow macaroni is best)
1 Tbsp. oil or margarine
1/3 lb. cheddar cheese, sliced

1 15-oz. can tomatoes, cut into
  chunks, juice reserved
salt and pepper to taste

Boil macaroni until tender; drain, and mix with oil or margarine. In a casserole, layer one-third of each ingredient as follows: macaroni, cheese slices, tomato chunks, salt and pepper. Repeat for a total of 3 times, ending with cheese and tomatoes. Pour reserved juice over the top. Bake, uncovered, at 375° for 40 minutes.

Shamburgers*

9-12 servings

1 c. dry garbanzo beans
¾ c. dry soybeans
1 c. water
2 Tbsp. tamari or soy sauce
1 medium onion, finely chopped
1 c. finely chopped celery

3 cloves garlic, minced
5 slices whole wheat bread,
  crumbled and dried
oil for frying
whole wheat buns, lettuce and
  tomato slices

Cover garbanzo beans and soybeans with water and soak, at least overnight. Do not cook.

Drain. Blend beans with 1 c. water in a food processor or blender until finely chopped. Do not drain. Add tamari, onion, celery and garlic. Shape into patties and dip in bread crumbs. Fry in a small amount of oil in a skillet over medium heat until golden brown on both sides, flipping halfway through.

Serve on whole wheat buns with lettuce and tomato slices.

Spaghetti For One*

1 serving

2 c. cooked spaghetti noodles,
  drained, still hot
1 Tbsp. oil
½ medium onion, finely chopped
1 clove garlic, minced
dash coarse black pepper

1 8-oz. can tomato sauce
½ tsp. oregano
1 tsp. marjoram
1 tsp. basil
1 tsp. cinnamon
1 Tbsp. dried parsley

Add onion and garlic to oil in frying pan over medium-low heat. Add pepper and saute until onion is tender. Turn off heat and mix in tomato sauce and remaining seasonings. Add spaghetti noodles and mix thoroughly. Let stand, covered, for 15-20 minutes before serving. Place over low heat if spaghetti is cooling too rapidly.

Stuffed Green Peppers*

2 servings

2 green peppers
½ c. brown rice
1¼ c. water
2 Tbsp. oil

1 medium onion, chopped
4 large mushrooms, chopped
2 medium tomatoes, chopped
salt and pepper to taste

Remove stems from green peppers and carefully scoop out insides through hole in top. Parboil, immersing in boiling water just until tender-crisp. Simmer rice and 1¼ c. water on low heat, covered, for 45-50 minutes. Turn off heat, remove lid and let stand for 5 minutes to dry out. Saute vegetables in oil for 5-10 minutes, until tender. Combine rice and vegetable mixture, season with salt and pepper, and use to stuff peppers.

Bake, covered, at 350° until hot.

I have from an early age abjured the use of meat, and the time will come when men such as I, will look upon the murder of animals as they now look upon the murder of men.

— Leonardo da Vinci

Szechwan Style Eggplant and Tofu *

6 servings

1 large eggplant, unpeeled,
  cut in ½x½x3-inch pieces
1/3 c. oil
1 tsp. salt
2 Tbsp. oil
2 large onions, chopped
1 Tbsp. fresh finely grated ginger root
2 Tbsp. minced garlic
2 small hot chilies (dried, from spice
  department), minced

5 Tbsp. soy sauce or tamari
3 Tbsp. vinegar
¾ c. water
1 Tbsp. sugar
1 tsp. sesame oil
2 Tbsp. cornstarch
¼ c. cold water
1 lb. tofu, cut in ¾-inch cubes
6 c. hot cooked rice

Heat 1/3 c. oil and salt in a wok or large frying pan to 375° (high). Carefully add eggplant and stir-fry for 12-15 minutes, or until the eggplant is soft and light brown but still intact. Remove eggplant and set aside.

Add 2 Tbsp. oil to hot wok and stir-fry the onions, ginger root, garlic and chilies until the onion is clear. Add the soy sauce, vinegar, ¾ c. water, sugar, and sesame oil and stir until heated to boiling. Add the cornstarch, dissolved in ¼ c. cold water, and heat to boiling, stirring. Add the eggplant and tofu and stir until thoroughly heated. Serve over hot rice.

This spicy hot dish can be made hotter or milder by varying the amount of hot chilies used.

Tofu-Vegetable Skillet Supper*

6-8 servings

3 Tbsp. oil
2 tsp. minced garlic
4 large carrots, in ⅛-inch slices
6 medium potatoes, scrubbed but
  not peeled, sliced lengthwise
  then cut in ¼-inch slices

¼ lb. mushrooms, sliced
1 10-oz. pkg. frozen peas
1 lb. firm tofu, drained and cut in
  ¾-inch cubes
½ tsp. cayenne (or less to taste)
2-3 Tbsp. soy sauce or tamari

Cook garlic in oil over medium heat in large frying pan about 1 minute. Increase heat to medium-high and add the carrots, potatoes, mushrooms and peas. Cook, stirring, 5-7 minutes. Cover and reduce heat to medium. Continue cooking, stirring occasionally, until potatoes are barely tender, about 20 minutes more. Do not overcook. Add tofu. Sprinkle with cayenne and soy sauce and cook, occasionally stirring gently, until tofu is heated through.

TVP Sloppy Joe*

2½-3 cups

1 c. TVP
1½ c. hot water
1 medium onion, chopped
2 Tbsp. oil
1½ c. catsup or a combination of 1 6-oz. can tomato paste, ¼ c. vinegar,
 ¾ c. water, 1 tsp. basil and ½ tsp. garlic powder

1 Tbsp. prepared mustard
2 Tbsp. molasses or other sweetener
salt to taste

Combine TVP and water. Let stand for 15 minutes. Meanwhile, saute onion in oil over medium-high heat until clear. In medium bowl, combine catsup or tomato paste mixture, mustard, molasses and salt. Add TVP when it is soft. Add TVP-catsup mixture to onions in frying pan. Simmer over medium heat for 15 minutes. This is good with dill pickles over whole wheat bread.

This spicy-hot dish can be made hotter or milder by varying the amount of hot chilies used.

Tofu Stew*

4 servings

2 Tbsp. oil
1 lb. firm tofu, drained and patted
 dry, then cut in small cubes
¼ c. tamari or soy sauce (tamari is
 best in this recipe)
1 clove garlic, minced
1 medium onion, chopped
2 carrots, cubed

2 medium potatoes, cubed
3 Tbsp. margarine
3 Tbsp. flour
½ tsp. coriander
½ tsp. basil
2 c. hot water
2 Tbsp. tamari or soy sauce
1 8-oz. can water chestnuts, drained

Heat 1 Tbsp. oil in a large skillet and saute tofu cubes over medium-high heat, stirring frequently, until lightly browned. Combine in a bowl with ¼ c. tamari and stir well. Set aside.

With the other 1 Tbsp. oil in the skillet saute the garlic, onions, carrots and potatoes for about 5 minutes, until just beginning to brown. Set aside.

In a Dutch-oven type pan, heat the margarine over medium heat. Stir in the flour with a whisk, then add the spices. When thickened and bubbly, add the hot water and 2 Tbsp. tamari. Stir with a whisk until smooth. Then add the tofu and its tamari, potatoes, onions, carrots, peas and water chestnuts. Simmer, covered, stirring occasionally, for another 20 minutes, adding small amounts of hot water if more gravy is desired.

Vegetable Chow Mein*

2-4 servings

4 c. water
1 5-oz. pkg. dry (not fried) chow
  mein noodles
4 Tbsp. oil
1 medium onion, chopped
2 stalks celery, diagonally sliced
  in ½-inch pieces
1 8-oz. can sliced water chestnuts,
  drained

1 carrot, thinly sliced on the diagonal
¾ c. frozen peas
1 c. bean sprouts
1-2 Tbsp. soy sauce or tamari
1 c. water or vegetable broth
1 Tbsp. cornstarch dissolved in
  1 Tbsp. water
salt and pepper

Cook chow mein noodles for 2 minutes in 4 c. boiling water. Do not overboil. Rinse under cold water and drain well.

Heat 2 Tbsp. oil in a wok or large frying pan. Add noodles and, stirring constantly, stir-fry for 4 minutes on medium-high heat. Remove and set aside.

Add 2 Tbsp. oil to wok. Stir-fry onion in the oil for 4 minutes, then add the remaining vegetables. Continue stir-frying until the celery just begins to become tender-crisp; only a few minutes. Add soy sauce and water and bring to a boil. Add cornstarch mixture and return to a boil, stirring. If a thicker sauce is desired, add additional cornstarch dissolved in water.

Stir in noodles and serve when heated through, seasoning with salt and pepper.

Adoption of a simple vegetarian diet would cut costs of the energy required to supply our food 80-95%, depending on how much cooking was involved.

— from "Vegetarianism for a World of Plenty"
Moneysworth Magazine, *March 1979*

Desserts

Here is a pretty good variety of recipes for cakes, pies, cookies, frostings, and even an "ice cream". What makes them different from the scores of other sweets you've concocted? They contain no dairy products or eggs.

For ideas on creating other vegan desserts, please consult "Baking Tips," p. 173.

---

*Banana Almond Cake**

One 9-inch cake

3 large very ripe bananas, mashed
    (about 1½ cups)
1 tsp. vanilla
½ c. oil
1½ c. sugar

2 c. flour
½ tsp. salt
1½ tsp. baking soda
½ c. (2 oz.) blanched slivered almonds

In a medium bowl stir together the bananas, vanilla, oil and sugar. Add the flour, salt and baking soda and stir to mix thoroughly. Spread in a greased and floured 9-inch round pan. (Do not use a smaller pan.) Sprinkle the almonds over the top.

Bake at 350° for 50 minutes, or until golden on top and a toothpick inserted in the center comes out clean. Cool before slicing and serving.

It often happens that the universal belief of our age, a belief from which no one was free or could be free without an extraordinary effort of genius or courage, becomes to a subsequent age so palpable an absurdity that the only difficulty is to imagine how such an idea could ever have appeared credible.

— *John Stuart Mill*

Note: An asterisk after the recipe title means the recipe is (or can be made) vegan, using no eggs or dairy products.

Banana-Tofu-Pineapple "Cheese"cake*

One 9-inch pie

Filling:
2 Tbsp. cornstarch
2 Tbsp. oil
2 Tbsp. water
½ c. brown sugar
2 Tbsp. lemon juice
1 tsp. grated lemon peel
1 tsp. cinnamon
1 tsp. vanilla
1 pkg. smooth tofu
3 medium-size, ripe bananas
1 can (8 oz.) crushed pineapple, well-drained

Graham Cracker Crust:
1 c. graham cracker crumbs
(Choose a lardless brand, such as Sunshine Honey Grahams®)
3 Tbsp. melted margarine

First, bake graham-cracker crust (see recipe above). In a blender, combine cornstarch, oil, water, sugar, lemon juice, lemon peel, cinnamon and vanilla. Drain tofu and pat dry. Break tofu and bananas into chunks. Gradually feed into blender as it whirls. Blend until smooth. Pour into bowl and stir in pineapple. Pour into cooked crust. Bake at 325° for 1 hour, or until center jiggles slightly.

To prepare crust, crush graham cracker crumbs using a rolling pin on a cutting board. Combine with margarine; mix with fork. Press into bottom of a pie plate or a 9-inch round pan with removable sides. Bake at 350° for 6 minutes; cool.

Variation: Omit graham cracker crust. Omit cornstarch, oil and water. Combine sugar, lemon juice, lemon peel, cinnamon and vanilla. Drain tofu and pat dry. Break tofu and bananas into chunks. Gradually feed into blender as it whirls. Blend until smooth. Pour into bowl and stir in pineapple. Pour into pie plate or a 9-inch round pan with removable sides. Freeze for 2 hours. Unmold and serve with sliced berries or kiwi fruit.

We tend to scoff at vegetarians, call them the nuts among the berries, but the fact is, they're doing much better than we are.

— *Dr. William Castelli*
Director of the federal government's
Framingham Heart Study in Massachusetts

Basic Pastry*

For single crust 9-inch pie

1 c. flour
½ tsp. salt

1/3 c. plus 1 Tbsp. vegetable shortening
2-2½ Tbsp. cold water

Mix flour and salt in a small bowl. Using a pastry blender or two dinner knives, cut in shortening until the mixture is crumbly. Add water, 1 Tbsp. at a time, and stir to blend well. If too little water is used the dough will be crumbly and will not hold together. If too much water is used the dough will be too sticky.

Gather dough into a ball and place on a well-floured work surface. Using a rolling pin, roll the dough into a circle about 11 inches in diameter, patching as necessary. Gently fold dough into quarters and place in a 9-inch pie pan. Unfold and smooth into pan, overlapping outer edge of pan slightly. Pinch crust around the rim to prevent shrinkage, and cut off excess crust.

If the recipe calls for the crust to be baked while empty, poke numerous holes in the crust (sides and bottom) before baking. This is not necessary if the crust will be filled before baking.

Brownies*

One 10-inch square pan

1/3 c. flour
1 c. water
½ c. margarine
2/3 c. cocoa
2 c. sugar

½ tsp. salt
1 tsp. vanilla
2 c. flour
2½ tsp. baking powder

Mix 1/3 c. flour with 1 c. water. Cook until thick and cool completely. Melt the margarine. Add the cocoa and stir until smooth. Cool. Beat the sugar, salt, and vanilla into the cooled flour mixture, then add the cocoa mixture. Mix together the 2 c. flour and baking powder and add to above ingredients. Bake in a 10″ square pan at 350° for 35 minutes or until an inserted knife comes out clean. This recipe makes a cakier brownie.

Variation: For fudge brownies, use ¾ c. cocoa and decrease flour mixture to 1½ c. flour and 2 tsp. baking powder.

Reprinted with permission from *The Farm Vegetarian Cookbook*, revised edition.

Circulation Bars*

36 bars

1½ c. molasses
3 Tbsp. oil
2 c. whole wheat flour
1 Tbsp. baking powder
peel of ½ orange, finely chopped
   or grated

1 Tbsp. cinnamon
1 Tbsp. ginger
½ tsp. cardamom
¼ tsp. ground cloves
1 c. sunflower seeds
1½-2 cups more whole wheat flour

In a large saucepan heat molasses and oil. Add 2 c. flour, baking powder, orange peel, spices and sunflower seeds. Add more flour until just sticky. Press mixture into a lightly greased 12x18-inch cookie pan.

Bake at 350° for 20-25 minutes. Cool and cut into bars.

Chocolate Chip Cookies*

4 dozen 3" cookies

1 c. margarine, softened
¾ c. sugar
¾ c. brown sugar
¼ c. water
1 tsp. vanilla

2¼ c. flour
½ tsp. salt
1 tsp. baking soda
1 pkg. (12 oz.) chocolate chips

Combine margarine, sugars, water, and vanilla in large bowl. Beat until creamy. Stir dry ingredients into mixture. Mix well. Form in 1¼" balls and flatten gently onto ungreased cookie sheets. Bake at 375° for 10-12 minutes.

Chocolate Cream Frosting*

2 cups — frosts tops and sides of two 9-inch cakes

6 Tbsp. margarine, softened
¾ c. cocoa
2 2/3 c. confectioners' sugar

¼ to 1/3 c. water
1 tsp. vanilla

Cream margarine in small mixer bowl. Add cocoa and confectioners' sugar alternately with water. Beat to spreading consistency. Additional water may be added. Blend in vanilla.

Crumb-Topped Apple Pie*

One 9-inch pie

Filling:
¾ c. sugar
¼ c. flour
1 tsp. nutmeg
2 tsp. cinnamon
dash salt
7 cups peeled, cored and thinly sliced
tart apples (7-8 medium apples)

Crust:
pastry for single crust 9-inch pie

Crumb Topping:
1 c. flour
½ c. margarine, chilled or partially
softened
½ c. brown sugar

To make filling, combine the ¾ c. sugar, ¼ c. flour, nutmeg, cinnamon and salt in a large bowl. Toss with apple slices until evenly distributed. Turn the apple mixture into unbaked pie crust in a 9-inch pie pan.

For crumb topping, cut the margarine into the 1 c. flour in a small bowl. Add brown sugar and stir until crumbly. Spread over apple filling, patting down lightly. Cover edge with 3-inch wide strips of aluminum foil to prevent burning.

Bake at 425° for 45 minutes, or until apples are barely tender and filling begins to bubble. About 30 minutes into baking, remove the edge foil strips to permit the edge of crust to brown lightly. If crumb topping is browning too rapidly place a sheet of aluminum foil loosely across the top of the pie for the last 15 minutes or so. Cool for several minutes before cutting and serving.

Date Oatmeal Squares*

One 8- or 9-inch pan

Date Filling:
2 c. chopped dates
2/3 c. water (or use half fruit juice,
half water)
2/3 c. sugar
1 tsp. lemon juice
½ tsp. grated lemon peel
2 Tbsp. margarine

Crust:
¾ c. margarine, softened
1 c. brown sugar, packed
1¾ c. sifted flour
½ tsp. baking soda
1½ c. quick cooking oats

For filling, combine all ingredients in a saucepan and cook over low heat, stirring frequently, until thickened (about 15 minutes). Cool.

For crust, cream together the softened margarine and brown sugar in a medium bowl. Sift together the flour and baking soda, then add the oats to the flour mixture. Combine the margarine mixture and flour mixture and stir to mix well.

Press half of the crust dough into an 8- or 9-inch square pan. Spread date filling over top. Sprinkle remaining crust evenly over filling and press down lightly.

Bake at 400° for 25-30 minutes. Cool and cut into squares.

Different Apple Pie*

One 9-inch pie

Filling:
6 Granny Smith apples
½ c. apple juice
½ c. honey or brown sugar
1 Tbsp. margarine
½ c. Kahlua®
1½ Tbsp. lemon juice
1½ Tbsp. cornstarch

Crust:
2 c. flour, white or whole wheat or
  a mixture
1 tsp. salt
2/3 c. vegetable shortening
1-3 Tbsp. water

Peel, core and slice apples into a large saucepan. Add juice and sugar and cook over medium heat until apples are almost tender. Remove with a slotted spoon. Add margarine and Kahlua® to cooking liquid. Combine lemon juice and cornstarch, add to liquid and cook over medium heat until smooth and thickened. Remove from heat; return apples to pan.

To prepare crust, combine flour and salt in a medium bowl. Cut in shortening until crumbly. Add the water 1 Tbsp. at a time, stirring, until dough holds together and is smooth. Roll out one-half of the dough on waxed paper. Fit into a 9-inch pie pan.

Fill crust with the apple mixture and cover with top crust. Brush with melted margarine and sprinkle with sugar. Cut 2-3 vent holes in top crust. Place on a cookie sheet to prevent bubble-over into oven.

Bake at 425° for 25-30 minutes.

Flaky Pastry*

Top and bottom crust for one 9" pie

3 c. flour
1½ tsp. salt
1 c. vegetable shortening

1 Tbsp. vinegar
6-8 Tbsp. ice water
⅛ tsp. baking powder

Mix flour and salt in a medium bowl. Add shortening and blend until the consistency of cornmeal, using a pastry blender or two dinner knives. Add the vinegar, water and baking powder. It will help to add the water one tablespoon at a time to ensure that you do not add too much. Work until the dough makes a nice firm ball. Roll out on a floured board.

Hearty Date-Carrot-Molasses Bars*

One 9-inch pan

½ c. cooked carrots
½ c. carrot cooking water
½ c. molasses
2 Tbsp. oil
¾ c. white flour
¾ c. whole wheat flour
½ tsp. cinnamon

½ tsp. nutmeg
½ tsp. baking soda
½ tsp. salt
1 c. chopped dates
1 c. chopped nuts (walnuts, pecans
   or almonds)

In a medium bowl beat together the carrots and water. Add molasses and oil, beating well. Add dry ingredients and stir to mix thoroughly. Stir in dates and nuts. Pat into a greased 9-inch square pan.

Bake at 350° for 30 minutes. Cool and cut into bars.

Karen's Cocoa Cake*

One 9x13-inch cake

3 c. flour
2 tsp. baking soda
½ tsp. salt
¾ c. cocoa
¾ c. margarine

2 c. sugar
¼ c. water
2 c. water, soymilk, or non-dairy
   liquid creamer
2 tsp. vanilla

Sift together the flour, soda, salt and cocoa. Set this aside while you cream the margarine. Gradually cream in the sugar. Add the water and beat well. Add the flour mixture alternately with the 2 cups of water or soymilk. Add vanilla and beat well.

Oil and flour a 9"x13" pan. Pour in the batter. Bake at 350° for 45 minutes or until an inserted toothpick comes out clean when you test the center.

Reprinted with permission from *The Farm Vegetarian Cookbook*, revised edition.

Four billion animals will be slaughtered for food in the United States this year.

— from "Vegetarianism for a World of Plenty"
Moneysworth Magazine, *March 1979*

Magic Chocolate Cake*

One 9-inch cake

1½ c. flour
1 c. sugar
½ tsp. salt
1 tsp. baking soda
3 Tbsp. cocoa

1 tsp. vanilla
1/3 c. oil
1 Tbsp. vinegar
1 c. cold water

Sift dry ingredients into a square baking pan (ungreased). Make three wells in flour. Pour vanilla, vinegar, and oil each in its well (one ingredient in one well). Pour water over all. Stir with a fork. Bake at 350° 30 minutes or until toothpick inserted in center comes out clean.

Nutty Apple Cake*

One 9x13-inch cake

¼ c. water
1/3 c. oil
4 c. apples, peeled, cored, and chopped
    into ¼-½-inch pieces (about 4 apples)
1½ c. sugar
1 tsp. vanilla

2 c. flour
1½ tsp. baking soda
½ tsp. salt
1½ tsp. cinnamon
1 c. chopped walnuts

In a medium bowl combine water, oil, apples, sugar and vanilla. Stir well. Add flour, baking soda, salt and cinnamon and mix thoroughly. Stir in walnuts. Batter will be very stiff. Spread in a greased and floured 9x13-inch pan.

Bake at 375° for 40 minutes, or until the top is golden and the cake is firm.

This cake is equally good for brunch or dessert.

Oatmeal Cookies*

4 dozen

½ c. margarine, softened
1/3 c. oil
1 c. brown sugar, packed
1 c. white sugar
1/3 c. soymilk or water
1 tsp. vanilla
2½ c. flour

1 tsp. baking soda
1 tsp. cinnamon
½ tsp. baking powder
1 tsp. salt
3 c. rolled oats
½ c. raisins (optional)

In a large bowl, cream margarine and oil together, then cream in sugars.

Add soymilk or water and vanilla. Beat until smooth. Beat in flour, baking soda, baking powder and salt. Mix, add oats and raisins, and blend in well. Drop rounded teaspoonsful onto ungreased cookie sheet.

Bake at 350° for 15 minutes or until the undersides just start turning brown.

Peanut Butter Cookies*

36 cookies

1 c. peanut butter
¾ c. margarine, softened
½ c. brown sugar, packed
½ c. sugar
1 tsp. vanilla
1 Tbsp. water

1 tsp. salt
1½ c. flour (replace ¼ c. with whole
    wheat flour if desired)
¾ tsp. baking soda
¾ tsp. baking powder

In a medium bowl cream the peanut butter, margarine and sugars. Stir in vanilla and water. Sift together the salt, flour, baking soda and baking powder, and add to the peanut butter mixture. Stir well. Roll into small balls and place on a greased cookie sheet. Flatten slightly with a fork dipped in flour.

Bake at 375° for 8-10 minutes, or until light golden underneath. Cool slightly before removing from cookie sheet.

Variation: Add up to ¾ c. chocolate chips to the creamed mixture before adding the dry ingredients. With chips included you will need to handle the dough carefully to keep the cookies together.

Poppyseed Cake*

One 9-inch loaf cake

1 c. boiling water
1 2-oz.jar (about ½ c.) poppyseeds
1¼ c. sugar
¾ c. margarine, softened

1 tsp. vanilla
½ tsp. salt
2 c. flour
2 tsp. baking powder

Pour boiling water over seeds in a small bowl. Let stand 30 minutes.

Mix sugar and margarine well. Add vanilla. Sift together the salt, flour and baking powder. Add to the sugar mixture and stir. Add poppyseed and water mixture and mix thoroughly. Spread in a well-greased and floured loaf pan.

Bake at 350° for 55 minutes, or until light golden on the outside and a toothpick inserted in the center comes out clean. Do not overbake. Let stand 5 minutes, then loosen sides carefully with a spatula and, handling very gently, turn out to cool.

Spice Cake*

One 9-inch cake

½ c. raisins
½ c. dates
1 c. white or brown sugar
1¾ c. water
½ tsp. salt
2 tsp. cinnamon

¾ tsp. nutmeg
¼ tsp. ground cloves
1 tsp. vanilla
2 c. flour
1 tsp. baking soda
1 tsp. baking powder

Combine first 8 ingredients in a large saucepan, bring to a boil, cook for 2 minutes, then cool to lukewarm. Add dry ingredients and vanilla. Mix well. Bake at 350° for 30 minutes in an oiled 9"x9" cake pan.

Spicy Pumpkin Pie*

One 9-inch pie

Filling:
¾ lb. firm tofu, drained and crumbled
   (1½ c.)
2¼ c. cooked or canned pumpkin
1 c. plus 2 Tbsp. sugar
1 Tbsp. oil
1 Tbsp. cinnamon

½ tsp. salt
½ tsp. ginger
¾ tsp. nutmeg
¼ tsp. ground cloves

Crust:
pastry for single crust 9-inch pie

Combine all filling ingredients in a blender and blend at high speed until smooth. Use a rubber spatula to push the ingredients down toward the bottom of the blender container repeatedly (with motor off). Pour into unbaked pie crust in a 9-inch pie pan.

Bake at 425° for 15 minutes, then reduce heat to 350° and bake 30 minutes more, or until a knife inserted in the center comes out clean. Cool before serving.

Super Fudge*

25 squares

1 c. honey
1 c. nut butter
1 c. carob powder
1 c. sesame seeds

1 c. sunflower seeds
½ c. shredded coconut
½ c. dates or other dried fruit, diced

Heat honey and nut butter over medium heat in a saucepan. Immediately add first the carob, and then the other ingredients. Stir to mix well.

Pour into a greased 8-inch square pan and refrigerate to harden. Cut into squares. Keep refrigerated.

Vanilla Tofu "Ice Cream"*

1 quart

½ c. oil
1 c. sugar
1 lb. tofu

1 c. soymilk or non-dairy liquid creamer (Mocha Mix® is good)
1 Tbsp. vanilla
pinch of salt

Blend all ingredients in blender until smooth. Freeze in an ice cream maker according to appliance directions.

Variation: Add ¼ c. cocoa to above ingredients to make chocolate "ice cream."

White Delight Frosting*

1 cup — frosts one 9x13-inch cake

¼ c. margarine, softened
2½ c. confectioners' sugar

1 tsp. vanilla (or ½ tsp. almond extract)
3 Tbsp. non-dairy liquid creamer or soymilk

Cream all ingredients together with an electric mixer. If too stiff to spread, add creamer, a teaspoonful at a time, and continue to mix until smooth.

People should consume . . . less saturated fat and cholesterol . . . less red meat . . . more complex carbohydrates such as whole grains, cereals, fruits, and vegetables.

*— **Healthy People**, a pamphlet*
by the U.S. Surgeon General
July 1979

"WILL THE REAL SAVAGE BEAST PLEASE <u>SIT DOWN</u> !"

Basics

This section discusses some unusual "basics" not found in typical American cookbooks. It will inform you about how to easily incorporate legumes, grains, soymilk, and gluten into your menu.

Soymilk

It is handy to know how to make soymilk because you can use it to replace milk in most recipes. It also makes very tasty eggless mayonnaise (see *Salad Dressing* section for recipe). It takes some time to make soymilk, but it's easy and inexpensive. Soybeans are available at co-ops and many natural food stores. If you're planning to adopt soymilk as a beverage, you might introduce yourself to the packaged, flavored varieties in the refrigerator section of your health food store or co-op. A couple of brands are Ah Soy® and Edensoy® They are more expensive then home-made soymilk, but they are very tasty, and can help you make the transition away from your customary "glass of moo." (Also at many natural food stores is soymilk powder, which you can easily convert to soymilk by following directions on the box.)

The following recipe makes about a quart of soymilk. You need a blender, a strainer, and a 4-quart pot. Start by rinsing one cup of dry soybeans. Soak overnight in the refrigerator in 3 cups of water. (You can speed the soaking process by pouring 3 cups of boiling water over the beans — they'll be ready in 2 hours). Drain the soaked beans and rinse again. Combine one cup of beans with three cups of water in the blender and blend for one minute until beans are ground very fine. Pour into pot and cook over medium heat. Repeat process with remainder of beans until all are added to the pot. Watch the cooking soymilk carefully — it foams and can boil over in just a second. After it has reached a boil, simmer for half an hour, stirring occasionally. Allow to cool slightly, then strain into a jar and refrigerate. You can make your own tofu by adding coagulant to the warm soymilk after straining. Instructions can be found in *Tofu Cookery, The Farm Vegetarian Cookbook,* and *Kathy Cooks Naturally,* to name a few. Information on these publications is on the *Cookbooks* page in the back of this book.

If you would like to use your soymilk as a beverage, add small amounts of salt, sugar or other sweetener, and vanilla until you get the taste you like. *Kathy Cooks Naturally* suggests that you can add calcium to soymilk by grinding a handful of sesame seeds along with the soaked beans, or blending tahini (sesame butter) with the finished milk.

Soymilk will stay fresh in the refrigerator for a week to 10 days. Try it in recipes for cake, cream soup, gravy, and pancakes (we have a soymilk pancake recipe in our *Breakfast* section). It can also be used along with tofu to make tofu "ice cream". See our recipe in the *Dessert* section. You'll probably be surprised at how little taste difference soymilk makes in recipes.

The pulp left over in the strainer is called okara or soy grits, and it has lots of uses. Incorporate it into your hot oatmeal at breakfast time. It's rich in protein and fiber. Adding one cup of okara to a 2-loaf bread recipe makes the bread moister, as well as contributing fiber, protein, and a little flavor. Consult *Kathy Cooks Naturally* and *The Farm Vegetarian Cookbook* for recipes too — "soy"sage, loaves, burgers, cookies, cakes, and muffins. Add ½ cup okara to your own recipes for the above foods. Okara should be stored in the refrigerator, and will last 10 to 14 days. It can also be frozen.

Who loves this terrible thing called War? Probably the meat eaters, who having killed, feel the need to kill . . . The butcher with his bloody apron incites bloodshed, murder. Why not? From cutting the throat of a young calf to cutting the throat of our brothers and sisters is but a step. While we are ourselves the living graves of murdered animals, how can we expect any ideal conditions on the earth?

— Isadora Duncan

Grains

"Whole-grain and bean cookery is one of the most pleasurable and important discoveries to be made by anyone newly turned vegetarian."[1]

There's quite a variety of grains that you can incorporate into your diet. Grocery stores sell rice, barley, cornmeal, and usually bulgur. Co-ops and natural food stores often sell grain in bulk — much cheaper. They carry additional selections like buckwheat, millet, whole wheat berries, and often other more exotic choices. Couscous and quinoa can be found at ethnic groceries.

This section will give you tips on preparing various grains. For ideas on herbs, spices and vegetables to add, look through our *Main Dish* and *Side Dish* chapters. Also consult *Laurel's Kitchen* and *The Moosewood Cookbook* (more information on our *Cookbook* page) for seasoning suggestions.

To cook a grain, rinse it with cold water. Bring water to a boil (amount will be specified in next paragraph). Pour in grain, adding ½ teaspoon of salt per cup of grain (adjust to your taste) and 1 tablespoon of margarine or oil (optional). Bring to a boil again, covered, and simmer until all water is

---

[1]Laurel Robertson, Carol Flinders, and Bronwen Godfrey, *Laurel's Kitchen*, (New York: Bantam Books in association with Nilgiri Press, 1976), p. 281.

absorbed and grain is tender. Most grains will triple in bulk when cooked. For each cup of brown rice, use 2 cups of water. Cook for one hour. Barley and millet require 3 cups of water for each cup of grain, and cook in about an hour. Buckwheat and bulgur cook in 15 minutes and you need 2 cups of water for each cup of grain. Cornmeal can be cooked as a grain (called polenta). Add 4 cups of water for each cup of cornmeal, and cook for 25 minutes. Wheat berries require 3 cups of water for each cup of grain, and cook in 2 hours.[2] Try mixing grains — a handful of wild rice or wheat berries along with brown rice, for example. Use the cooking instructions for rice.

Cooked grains will keep in the refrigerator for about a week. You can cook a large amount to store, warming up small portions as needed. Top grain with beans and/or vegetables for a quick meal. Turn to the *Vegetarina* chapter for particulars. Leftovers can be added to soups or casseroles.

Legumes

Beans look pretty in jars in your kitchen, and they taste great, too. When served with grains, they provide a complete protein source (though protein is rarely a problem for vegetarians or vegans — see our section entitled *A Word about Protein*).

Cooking beans is similar to cooking grain, except it usually takes longer. Beans will double their volume when cooked. First, look for rocks in the beans. Then, rinse well. Add water to beans in a pot, cover, bring to a boil, reduce heat, and simmer until beans are tender. Add salt at the point they are tender, again ½ teaspoon per cup of dry beans, or suit yourself.

Lentils, split peas, and black-eyed peas take the shortest time to cook — one hour. They require 3 cups water per cup of dry beans.

Black beans, kidneys, limas, baby limas, and navy beans cook in 1½ hours. Use 4 cups of water per cup of black beans, 3 for kidneys, and 2 for limas, baby limas, and navy beans.

Great northerns and pintos cook in about 2½ hours and require 3 cups water for each cup dry beans.

Garbanzos and red beans take 3 hours to cook and each cup of beans needs 3 cups water.

Soybeans require 3 cups of water per cup of beans. They usually take longer than 3 hours to cook. *Laurel's Kitchen* suggests you can reduce cooking time by half an hour or so by soaking the beans overnight in the refrigerator before cooking — a trick that works on all legumes.[3]

Another way to cook beans is in a slow cooker. Bring beans and water to a boil on high (2 cups water for each cup beans — any assortment of beans will work). Then turn to low and simmer about 8 hours — even soybeans cook thoroughly this way. This is easy to do overnight and you can wake up to a hearty beans-and-bread breakfast.[4] Or you can store the

[2]Robertson, *Laurel's Kitchen*, p. 288.

[3]Robertson, *Laurel's Kitchen*, p. 286.

[4]Robertson, *Laurel's Kitchen*, p. 121.

cooked beans in the refrigerator to warm up as needed (they keep for about a week). Again, we haven't mentioned seasonings here, but check our recipe chapters for ideas, as well as *Laurel's Kitchen, The Moosewood Cookbook,* and *The Enchanted Broccoli Forest* (see *Cookbooks* in the back of this book for more information.)

You ask me why Pythagoras abstained from eating meat. For my part, I wonder what was the disposition, idea or motive of the first man who put to his mouth a thing slaughtered and touched to his lips the flesh of a dead animal . . .

— *Plutarch*
from **The Eating of Meat**

Gluten

Gluten is a mixture of wheat flour, water, and seasonings that can replace meat in many traditional recipes. For brands of gluten commercially available, check our *Meat Substitutes* chapter.

To make gluten, put 7 cups of whole wheat flour in a large bowl. Add 2½ to 3 cups of water and shape into a ball. Cover with 4 more cups of water. Set aside for at least 20 minutes but no more than 4 hours. When you are ready, gently knead the ball of flour while it is submerged in the water. This separates the starch and bran from the gluten. The water will become very thick with the starch and bran. Pour it off (you might want to save it to use as a thickener or to make into a breakfast cereal). Add another quart of water to the gluten and knead once again until the water is thick and starchy. Pour this off just like before. Repeat, adding more water and continuing to knead until the water is reasonably clear. You now have approximately 2 cups of gluten.

What to do with Starch and Bran Left Over from Gluten Making

1. Toss it out.
2. After the water separates and becomes clear, carefully pour it off. Stir sediment and pour onto cookie sheet to air dry (or put in oven at very low temperature). When it's dry, crumble and then blend until it's a powder. Use as a thickener.
3. Pour off water as you would when making a thickener. Add one tablespoon yeast and 2 tablespoons sugar or other sweetener to ¼ cup of warm water. Stir into starch and bran mixture. Let stand for 30 minutes. Pour onto 3 oiled cookie sheets and let it stand 30 more minutes. Bake at 275° for 2 hours. Remove from oven. When cool, crumble into small pieces. This can now be eaten like a breakfast cereal — sort of like Grape Nuts.

Gluten "Chicken"

2 c. gluten
3 c. water
1 Tbsp. nutritional yeast
½ tsp. salt
½ tsp. celery seed
¼ tsp. sage
¼ tsp. thyme

½ tsp. cumin
½ tsp. coriander
¼ tsp. garlic powder
¼ tsp. tarragon
¼ tsp. rosemary
½ tsp. turmeric
2 tsp. corn oil

Divide gluten into 8 pieces. With mallet or knife, pound into cutlet shapes. Put water in pan with all of the spices and the oil. Bring to a near boil. Place gluten pieces into this simmering broth, and cook for 40 minutes. Do not boil. Remove gluten from broth. Drain and cool. This can be used in many traditional American dishes. It can be diced into salads, breaded and fried, or eaten cold in sandwiches.

"NOW I KNOW WHY THEY CALL HIM THE GALLOPING GOURMET."

Gluten "Roast"

1½ c. water
¾ tsp. pepper
¼ tsp. onion powder
3 Tbsp. tamari soy sauce

2 tsp. ground cumin
1 tsp. ground coriander
2 c. gluten

In a slow cooker, add spices to water. Shape gluten into a ball, place in slow cooker. Cook for 16 hours on low, basting occasionally. Slice "roast" and serve with gravy (the broth the gluten simmered in makes a good gravy when thickened with oil and flour), or slice into sandwiches.

Seawheat (Gluten "Clams")

½ c. seaweed (dulse, kombu or wakame)
3 c. water
1 Tbsp. sugar or other sweetener
½ tsp. salt

1 Tbsp. oil
2 Tbsp. lemon juice
2 c. gluten

Tear seaweed into one-inch pieces. Add water, spices and oil. Bring to a gentle boil. Add gluten by teaspoonsful. Remove each piece when it rises to the top of the water (about 3 minutes).

"I have just endured one of the most cold sweat experiences of my life. I heard the 'voice of an animal'." Paul Harvey, commenting on the 'words' of Washoe, the 15 year old chimpanzee who has learned sign language in a research project at the University of Oklahoma. "When she was able to put words together on her own into a phrase — these were her first three. And she has said them again repeatedly to visitors. The voice from the cage is saying: 'Let me out'."

"Vegetarina," Fast and Easy

No, it is not true! To eat vegetarian, one need not spend an hour or two of preparation per meal. There are fast and easy meals you can prepare all by yourself, with minimum trouble, and without loss of daylight hours. Sometimes you may sacrifice the goodness of fresh foods in preference for the convenience of some "instant" packaged foods (such as rice and potatoes), but for those who loathe the kitchen, the trade-off may well be worthwhile. We present here a few ideas. Now remember — this is the "fast" method; these recipes aren't too hard, neither are they too specific. Use your tastes as a guide to spice and thicken and mix. No rules —except: Please yourself.

One type of quick and hearty meal involves variations of SAUCE with VEGETABLES mixed in, which is then poured over a CARBOHYDRATE FOOD. If you eat cheese, you may wish to add a couple slices where it sounds appealing.

SAUCE:

The easiest sauces are canned soups. Creamed soups like celery or mushrooms are versatile. Tomato soup, as well as tomato sauce or paste, also is very useful. (Remember, tomato paste is the "purest" of these three, having no added spices. You spice according to your taste. Also, it's more concentrated; a little will take you further.) Be sure to note the ingredient label of creamed soups; many of them contain animal ingredients, even though the soup itself is cream of "vegetable."

Heat the soup with only a little dilution, depending on how thick you want your sauce. You may spice the sauce in a variety of ways, but garlic, we advise, is a must. Cumin and curry are both good spices to add to a tomato sauce. To spice up mushroom soup, you can try a dash of lemon juice or tabasco, and maybe a little coriander — or leave as is. Salt and pepper to taste. A chopped *onion* (sauteed first, if desired) is a recommended addition, especially to sauce with a tomato base.

Feedlots and slaughterhouses are responsible for more of the nation's water pollution than all of industry and households combined.

— from "Vegetarianism for a World of Plenty"
Moneysworth, March 1979

VEGETABLES

Quick and easy means frozen or canned to most people. Peas, or a carrots and peas blend, green beans, and corn are easiest, but try anything — lima beans, brussel sprouts, broccoli, cauliflower. If frozen, make sure they are thawed and heated through before eating them; the larger vegetables will take longer. We should note that if you can stand to add the simple step of steaming fresh vegetables to your routine rather than using canned or frozen vegetables, you'll be adding to the taste and nutritional value of your meal. *Vegetables are put into sauce to heat.*

CARBOHYDRATE

Your choice. Potatoes (mashed, fried, boiled; instant or fresh), toast, noodles (macaroni, spaghetti; flat, regular, wheat, spinach...), rice, etc. Follow package instructions to prepare. *Vegetable and sauce mixture is poured over carbohydrate.*

Here are a few examples:

1. Time yourself. Take two pans. Boil noodles (according to package directions) in the first pan. In the second, heat mushroom soup with a little water. Add peas to soup (and please, some garlic). Finally, pour the sauce over the drained noodles. Salt to taste.

2. How about this? Fry slices of potatoes until tender and crisp. In a separate pan, make your sauce from tomato soup (or sauce or paste) — heating with a little water, garlic, cumin, curry powder, and salt and pepper (use all spices to your taste). Add to sauce green beans, peas, or corn (or all of them, if you like). Simmer. A chopped onion can either be added to the sauce, or fried up with the potatoes. Pour sauce over potatoes. This sauce is good over mashed potatoes or rice, too (and these you can buy in a box).

3. Or, stepping up to fresh vegetables... slice zucchini and onion. Fry together until tender. Add the tomato sauce with cumin, garlic and curry powder. Serve over mashed potatoes. As always, salt and pepper to taste.

4. Getting just a little more complicated...

   — Chop an onion and fry in oil. While onion is frying, cube half an eggplant. When onion is getting tender, add eggplant and fry until soft (it doesn't take long!).

   — Soak approximately 1/3 c. TVP (see Soymeat and Gluten section) in about ½ c. water and a dash of vinegar for about 5 minutes.

   — Add to all of this the same tomato sauce mixture (sauce, cumin, curry, garlic, salt and pepper); spice and thicken to your taste.

   Eat over mashed potatoes, rice, etc. The total dish takes about 15 minutes to prepare, and it's really good!

Other Ideas

- Spicy Cabbage. Chop cabbage (purple is pretty) and fry in oil with turmeric, a little cayenne, and salt. Careful with the cayenne — this can get pretty hot. Serve with sandwiches, or potatoes, or flat noodles on the side.

- Simple Chole. Chop one onion. Simmer one 15-oz. can tomato sauce. Add onion and one can garbanzo beans to sauce. Spice with cumin and curry powder. Serve with rice. (For an added flavor, mix peanut butter with cooked rice. Serve rice on side. Again, this tastes better than it sounds, and it's especially good with chole).

- Eggplant and onion makes a great and quick burger. See page 141.

- Salad. Don't forget the obvious. Salad is variable and salad is good for you. Mix different kinds of lettuce, spinach and sprouts — using sunflower seeds, almond slices, croutons, tomatoes, avocado, artichoke hearts, mushrooms, olives, bacon bits. See salad section (p. 95) for more ideas.

- Sloppy Joe. See page 147 for this easy recipe.

- Soup and Sandwich. The old standby. You can make your own quick soup with vegetable broth (mixes listed on p. 21), or miso. Add peas, cabbage and mushrooms. Spread some peanut butter, or place sliced cheese on bread. Broil in oven for a toasted, open-face sandwich. See sandwich section (p. 107) for good ideas.

- Soy "meat" can be adapted as a meat substitute right into your former fast-food menu. There are grillers (hamburger patty substitute), bacon substitutes, and sausage substitutes available in almost any supermarket. A larger variety of meat substitutes, such as imitation lunchmeats, steaklets, hot dogs, and more are available in most health-food stores. See Soymeat and Gluten, page 77, for more detailed information.

- Spaghetti and cabbage. Sounds bad, tastes good. Chop ½ medium-size cabbage and one medium onion. Sautee in margarine and garlic. Be liberal with both. Boil enough spaghetti (or macaroni noodles) for about 2 servings. When cabbage and onion are tender, mix with drained spaghetti. Flavor with soy sauce.

- Packaged Ramen (the kind with no animal flavorings; check ingredients). To make more hearty, add chopped Chinese (napa) cabbage, peas, mushrooms, etc.

- Spaghetti is easy, especially when you buy prepared sauce. Add sauteed mushrooms, and if you'd like, TVP (see page 78).

- Tacos. Keep your can of vegetarian refried beans nearby (see p. 21) and stock up on shells. You've got your chopped tomato, avocado, onion, lettuce and sauce (as well as grated cheese if you eat it). Need we say more? One nice addition is sauteed mushrooms, chopped and mixed in with the refried beans.

• Use firm tofu. Slice. Mix a little flour and garlic powder together; dip tofu in mixture until coated. Fry tofu in a little oil and soy sauce until browned on outside. Fry some onion slices along with it. Eat in sandwich or along with vegetable on the side.

100,000,000 gallons of water is used every day by just 1 chicken processing plant — that's enough to service a community of 25,000 people.

— from "Food Price Rises"
by Sylvia Porter
New York Post

Suggestions and Tips

At least know how to boil a potato. You can boil several on Sunday and have them handy in the refrigerator (with skins on) for use throughout the week. Also, have a vegetable steamer on hand, and when you can, indulge in fresh vegetables — don't get *too* accustomed to the packaged variety. It's this simple: ¾ inches water at the bottom of the pan. Place the steamer basket in the pan, and your choice of vegetable. Cover pan and bring to a boil. Cook to desired degree of tenderness. This method is quicker than boiling, and nutrients and flavor remain *in* your food, rather than leaching into water.

Check chapter titled Hidden Slaughterhouse and Dairy Products in Food, pages 19-29, for lists of vegetarian packaged foods. But to give you an idea, the following can be bought vegetarian and in a convenient form: Instant rice and mashed potatoes, macaroni and cheese in a mix, canned vegetarian cheese ravioli. Heinz makes vegetarian baked beans. Garbanzo beans and canned soups are useful to have on hand, as are packaged noodles and salad dressing. Remember that blackeyed peas and kidney beans also come in a can, and salsa and chips are on the shelf with popcorn and peanuts for snacks and travel food.

Raw food. Yes, you don't want packaged — you can still get it raw. Remember raisins, nuts, and raw fruits and vegetables; as well as drained fruits with crackers on the side. All are quick, easy and good tasting lunch, breakfast, and snack fare that we suggest you keep stocked up on. And, lucky you, your health is not likely to suffer from eating them.

One other suggestion: To add more variety to your quickie diet, explore a few different grains that you may not be used to. For example, couscous can be purchased in box form at most grocery stores (or in bulk from some co-ops). It's easy to prepare and pleasing to the palate when prepared with margarine, peas, and sauteed mushrooms. Next, to make you feel really good about yourself, you can branch out into bulgur.

Vegetarianism is easy to adapt into any lifestyle, once you've decided to make the initial adjustment. As with any diet, to keep it interesting and your meals more appealing, the trick is to allow yourself to explore a little. Even with quick and easy meatless meals, you don't have to get into a rut. Look for variety, try variety. It is helpful in the beginning to make a list of the meals available to you — the ones you like — so that in the future, only a minimum amount of time has to be spent planning, shopping, and cooking. Please also check through our other recipe sections, as you will probably find many other dishes easy enough and quick enough to suit your lifestyle. If, in your quest for the quick and flavorful menu, you develop favorites you would like to share, please mail them to PAWS and we will try to include your contribution in later editions of this book.

How can I teach your children gentleness and mercy to the weak and reverence for life, which in its nakedness and excess, is still a gleam of God's omnipotence, when by your laws, your actions and your speech, you contradict the very things I teach?

— Henry Wadsworth Longfellow

Baking Tips

Adapting your favorite baked goods recipes to vegan cooking may be as simple as switching from lard to vegetable shortening, or as challenging as coming up with a substitute for cream cheese.

Expect some changes in texture; and expect both successes and failures when experimenting. With that in mind, it's probably best to perfect the recipe before an important culinary occasion arises.

When modifying a recipe, be sure to write down each change you make, so if it works well you'll be able to replicate it. And if it doesn't, you'll know what not to do the next time.

Eggs

Commercial egg-replacers, or egg-substitutes, are available in most health food stores. These come in powdered form and are totally egg-free, in contrast to refrigerated egg substitutes such as Egg Beaters. Powdered replacers will compensate for eggs as ingredients in other dishes, but cannot be used in omelets, scrambled, or otherwise substituted in recipes which use eggs in starring roles.

If the original recipe calls for several eggs, attempts to make the recipe eggless are less likely to succeed than similar recipes which call for fewer eggs.

Most packaged egg-replacer directions call for one teaspoon of powdered egg-replacer for each egg omitted. You may have more success using more — about one tablespoon, plus one tablespoon water, per egg. If the batter or dough is very dry, slightly increase the amount of water added; but don't add more than one additional tablespoon per egg.

Either arrowroot powder (available in health food stores) or cornstarch (which is cheaper) works very well as egg replacers in many cookies, breads and other pastries. Use one tablespoon of either, plus one tablespoon water, to replace each egg. Either stir together the cornstarch or arrowroot and water before adding this mixture to the dough, or simply add each separately. Again, you may need to increase the amount of water if you're working with dry dough, but don't over do it.

Cornstarch or arrowroot works well as egg-replacer in main dish loaves (soy, nut, vegetable), too. Plan to cook the dish longer than the recipe indicates. A less-than-firm loaf can always be shaped into patties and fried.

Another easy substitute you might wish to try in baked goods is ¼ cup of tofu to replace each egg in a recipe. The tofu will firm up the baked product. It can be blended with the liquid ingredients before adding them to the rest of the recipe.

Milk

Many baked goods and frostings work perfectly if you substitute an equal amount of water for the milk required. Soy milk also works well and will increase the nutritional value of the dish. If using powdered soy milk, just add the powder along with the dry ingredients and add the necessary amount of water at the point in the recipe when milk would usually be added. Consult package directions for the amount of powdered soy milk to use for each cup of water. Non-dairy liquid creamers are also good milk or cream substitutes in many recipes.

It takes 5 acres of land to feed 1 American. It takes ¼ acre of land to feed 1 Egyptian.

— *from "Vegetarianism for a World of Plenty"*
Moneysworth Magazine, *March 1979*

Butter

Vegan margarine or solid vegetable shortening will substitute for butter or lard in any recipe. For rich flavor use either margarine or butter-flavored vegetable shortening. The combination of half margarine and half butter-flavored solid shortening works very well in cookie dough.

If using either solid shortening or regular stick margarine as a replacement for butter or lard, use the same amount of shortening called for in the recipe.

"Light" margarines are lower in fat and calories than regular margarine or butter and also contain more water. To bake with a "light" margarine use 1¼ cups to replace 1 cup of regular shortening, and decrease the amount of liquid added by three tablespoons. If the recipe doesn't call for any added liquid you won't be able to reduce the liquid, so regular margarine will probably produce better results.

The buttery flavor that makes croissants and fillo pastries delicious can be closely duplicated using a soy margarine in stick form (Nucoa® is especially good). For croissants, substitute margarine for butter in the dough. Replace the beaten egg mixture brushed over the tops with melted margarine to which one teaspoon of buttery flavored popcorn popping oil has been added. Baking time and temperature will be the same. The melted butter needed in fillo recipes can be replaced with melted margarine with one teaspoon of buttery flavored popcorn oil mixed in for every ½ cup of margarine used.

Cookies

Most drop and bar cookies work well using cornstarch or arrowroot (one tablespoon, plus one tablespoon water per egg) to replace eggs. Or use ¼ cup tofu to replace each egg, beaten into the shortening and sugar.

Brownies are a peculiar exception: use the recipe we've provided (p. 151) instead of trying to adapt your favorite unless you have ample time, cocoa and patience.

Since eggs serve as binders, holding the ingredients together, the cookie dough may literally crumble without them. This problem is easily solved by shaping the dough into a log shape, wrapping tightly in waxed paper and refrigerating a few hours until firm. Then peel off the wrapper, slice and bake the dough as for refrigerator cookies. For an average sized drop-type cookie use a log about 2 inches in diameter. Cut in ¾-inch thick slices, then cut each slice into quarters.

If you're in too much of a hurry to wait for the dough to chill, you can achieve the same results by shaping the individual cookies by hand. Working with 1/3 to 1/2 cup dough at a time, use both cupped hands to squeeze the clump of dough until it adheres together and is smooth on the outside. It doesn't matter what the shape of the dough is at this point; the important thing is to form it into a solid, cohesive mass. Next, pinch off enough dough for one cookie and form into the desired shape. If the directions call for the dough to be flattened with the bottom of a glass or a fork, do this gently or the cookie may fall apart.

Many cookies become tougher if baked without eggs, so it's a good idea to shorten the baking time slightly. Another common problem in dairyless cookies is a too-greasy result. When an option is given, use a little extra flour to avoid this. And the tofu trick will help here, as well.

If in doubt about whether a cookie recipe can go eggless (most can, using water and arrowroot or cornstarch instead) make the dough and cook one or two test cookies. If they aren't what you wanted you can add more arrowroot or cornstarch and try again, add a little extra flour, shorten cooking time, or press into a greased pan and make bar cookies. These may take a while to cook, but they usually turn out nice and chewy.

Formerly, people said: Who is your neighbor? Man. Today we must no longer say that. We have gone further and we know that all living beings on earth who strive to maintain life and who long to be spared pain — all living beings on earth are our neighbors.

— *Albert Schweitzer*

Unyeasted Breads and Cakes

These are most easily adapted to vegan cooking if the intended texture of the finished product is moist and rather heavy. Many breads (some banana, pumpkin, and zucchini recipes, for example) work well if the eggs are simply omitted. Cakes and other breads will usually need cornstarch or arrowroot in place of the eggs. If the batter is quite moist try adding one tablespoon cornstarch or arrowroot to replace each egg without adding extra water. Or again, blend ¼ cup of tofu into the liquid ingredients for each egg being replaced.

Pies, Tarts and Quiches

Most fruit pies are vegan as long as vegetable shortening is used in the crust.

Custard-type fillings and puddings can be made using a blended tofu base and soy milk in place of eggs and milk or cream. See *Tofu Cookery* or *The Farm Vegetarian Cookbook* for a great selection of recipes of this type.

A dairy-free quiche can be made using tofu as a main ingredient. For a 9-inch quiche, use 2 lbs. of tofu. Combine in a blender with 1 cup of non-dairy liquid creamer, soymilk or broth. Add a tablespoon of cornstarch (to help it set), a quarter teaspoon of turmeric (to give a golden color), and 2 teaspoons of baking soda (to make it rise). Saute a combination of two or three vegetables (mushrooms, spinach, and onions are great) and add herbs (pepper, basil and garlic work well) and a teaspoon of salt. Mix well with the tofu mixture, pour into an unbaked piecrust, and bake at 375° for one hour.

"SO I TOLD MY COUSIN SID: 'LISTEN, SID. FORGET HUMANE. FORGET HEALTHY. IF IT TASTES GOOD, I EAT IT.'"

The Vegetarian Pet

The dilemma: You're a vegetarian pet owner doing all you can to minimize animal exploitation in your lifestyle, but what is it that your dogs and cats jump up and down for at 5:00? Canned animals. Pelletized animals. Granulated animals. Pet food. How can you feel good about feeding one animal to another, especially knowing that the animals in that pet food probably endured a lousy life? Is there an alternative? Can dogs and cats be vegetarian?

Well, gathering the wisdom of experience and literature together, the consensus on that question is "yes, definitely" for dogs, and "yes, with some cheating" for cats. For a more in-depth coverage of this topic, we refer you to an excellent book, *Dr. Pitcairn's Complete Guide to Natural Health for Dogs and Cats* by Richard H. Pitcairn and Susan Hubble Pitcairn. It can be ordered from the Progressive Animal Welfare Society, P.O. Box 1037, Lynnwood, WA 98046. Pitcairn's book provides detailed and documented information on the health and care of companion animals, along with a variety of pet food recipes you can make easily at home.

Dogs

In the meantime, however, we would like to turn things over to the voice of experience and let a local couple with six vegetarian dogs tell you how they do it, and how their dogs like it. Karen and Les use a breakfast and dinner recipe adapted from Pitcairn's book. Since they have so many dogs, they prepare the dinner in bulk. For less populated households, the food can be frozen indefinitely or refrigerated for about a week. Meals should be served at room temperature for best digestion. These recipes are followed by a feeding chart from Pitcairn's book.

80-90 percent of U.S. grains and legumes and more than half of the cropland is used to feed livestock which consumes up to 80 pounds of vegetable protein to produce one pound of animal protein, while 800 million people on this planet are on the verge of starvation.

— *Veg. Information Service*

Dog Breakfast

Single serving for a 25-lb. dog

1½ c. cooked oatmeal (rolled oats, not quick oats)
1 c. whole milk

The oatmeal can be cooked the night before so it has reached room temperature by breakfast time. Add milk and serve.

"CATS AND DOGS! FIGHTING AGAIN! LIKE CATS AND DOGS!"

Dog Dinner

Single serving for a 25-lb. dog

2½ oz. tofu or ¼ c. cooked soy grits
2 eggs, scrambled (preferably from
free-running chickens), or ½ c.
    cottage cheese
¾ tsp. oil

Mix together and serve.

2 c. cooked brown rice or 2 c. of any of
    the following cooked grains: barley,
    bulgur, millet, or cornmeal
½ to ¾ c. chopped or grated vegetables
    (raw is great, steamed is okay)

Bulk Dog Dinner

Yields 18 cups

1 lb. tofu or 1½ c. cooked soy grits
1 dozen eggs, scrambled (preferably
from free-running chickens), or 3 c.
    cottage cheese
2 Tbsp. oil

12 c. cooked brown rice or 12 c. of any
    of the following cooked grains:
    barley, bulgur, millet, or cornmeal
3 to 4 c. chopped or grated vegetables
    (raw is great, steamed is okay)

Mix together and serve. May be frozen or refrigerated.

Weight Feeding Guide — Dogs
(daily nutrition requirement)

Dog's weight	Multiply single dinner and breakfast recipe by:
5 lbs	¼
10 lbs	½
15 lbs	¾
25 lbs	1
32 lbs	1¼
40 lbs	1½
60 lbs	2
85 lbs	2½
105 lbs	3
125 lbs	3½
150 lbs	4

Karen and Les, who say their dogs prefer this diet to their old one, offer the following tips:

1. To cut costs, buy grains and whole powdered milk at co-ops. Buy whatever vegetables are the cheapest. Carrots can be purchased at feed stores for very little.

2. More food value is retained in raw vegetables, which can be grated or chopped. Frozen vegetables can also be used. Add boiling water to them to thaw; cooking is not necessary.

3. When possible, vary the grains and vegetables with each batch of food you make to provide a well-rounded diet.

4. Try serving the breakfast recipe to replace the dry food your dog has been used to munching on during the day. Raw carrots, apples and cauliflower can take the place of bones in keeping your pet's teeth nice and clean.

And the best testimony? "No finicky eaters anymore. The dogs like this diet and everyone's weight has stabilized, bringing our two underweight and our two overweight dogs to where they should be. And what's good for us is that in the year-and-a-half that our dogs have been on this diet, we have made fewer trips to the vet. With six dogs, that adds up to a real moneysaver."

If your dog doesn't immediately take to a vegetarian diet, don't give up. Try working the new foods gradually into his/her old diet. This will allow him/her to become accustomed to the change and adapt his taste to something new. Dogs can get hooked on foods they had previously turned their meat-eating noses up at, as one vegetarian pet owner whose canine companion now loves garbanzo beans can attest to.

Pitcairn suggests that dogs on vegetarian diets receive the following supplements:

Dog Powder Mix

2 c. nutritional yeast
1½ c. bonemeal (can substitute 1 c. dicalcium phosphate — made from rock and available in pet stores — as bonemeal really is ground up bones)
½ c. kelp powder.

Store mixture in a sealed bottle on a dark shelf.

Dog Oil Mix

1¾ c. vegetable oil
¼ c. cod-liver oil

50-100 IU vitamin E (to prevent spoilage)

Keep mixture refrigerated in a sealed bottle.

Never to blend our pleasure or pride with sorrow of the meanest thing that feels.

— *William Wordsworth*

Amount of Supplement to Feed Daily

Weight	Powder	Oil	Vitamin E (measured in IU) In addition to that in the oil mix
5-15 lbs	2 tsp.	1 tsp.	50
15-30 lbs	4 tsp.	2 tsp.	100
30-50 lbs	2 Tbsp.	1 Tbsp.	150
50-80 lbs	3 Tbsp.	1½ Tbsp.	200
80-110 lbs	¼ c.	2 Tbsp.	300
100+ lbs	1/3+.c.	2½+ Tbsp.	400

The powder and oil can be included in the recipes, but the oil will not stay fresh too long when mixed with food (three or four days in the refrigerator is okay); or they can be added to the food along with the vitamin E at mealtime.

Commercial dog vitamins are available, but don't be surprised to find animal ingredients in most of them.

There are just a few vegetarian dog foods beginning to appear on the market. Nature's Recipe® makes kibble and canned dog food which is actually vegan*. It can be special ordered at the Minglement on Vashon Island (see p. 53 for address and phone number), and other health-food stores and co-ops may start selling it soon. Call your co-op; your voice might be the one that convinces them to stock vegetarian pet food. It can also be purchased by mail from these addresses:

Nature's Recipe
P.O. Box 5249
Orange, CA 92667
(714) 639-1134

Kathy Nelson
c/o Nelson Hardware
7425 N. Leavitt
Portland, OR 97223
(503) 246-0854

Amberwood
Rt. 1, Box 206
Milner, GA 30257
(404) 358-2991

Don't have regrets about taking things one step at a time. Even reducing your pet's meat consumption is an achievement.

Farms like the one of my childhood are rapidly being replaced by animal factories. Animals are reared in huge buildings, crowded in with cages stacked up like so many shipping crates. On the factory farm there are no pastures, no streams, no seasons, not even day and night. Animal-wise herdsmen and milkmaids have been replaced by auto-mated feeders, computers, closed-circuit television and vacuum pumps. Health and productivity come not from frolics in sunny meadows but from syringes and additive-laced feed.

— Jim Mason
Attorney and Author of
Animal Factories

---

*Except for its vitamin D3, derived from lanolin, which comes from sheep's wool.

Cats

There is more disagreement as to whether a cat can make a good vegetarian than there is over dogs. It is generally agreed that dogs are fine vegetarians. Cats may not be. Dr. Pitcairn says that with some cod-liver oil supplement, a cat can do fine, but advises (to be perfectly safe) occasionally feeding your feline pet a small amount of fish or meat.

It also seems to be harder to get a cat to make the transition to a vegetarian diet, but here again are some personal accounts and tips that may help your cat eat less carnivorously.

Leanne and Haley are vegetarians who had two stray cats show up a week apart at their doorstep.

"We had no meat or dairy products in the house and were loath to support any slaughterhouse industry. These cats were not choosy, however, as they came to us hungry. Our first offerings were things like brown rice, cornmeal, bread with nutritional yeast, tomatoes, eggplant, and lentils. They ate them all contentedly and with relish. However, we felt that if they were going to stay with us, we'd better do what we could to make sure they were getting the best we could give them. We now usually work around variations of a vegetarian recipe for cats in the Pitcairn book, which is as follows:"

Dairy Delight for Cats

1 tsp. oil
1 medium egg, scrambled (if no free-running chicken eggs are available, you may substitute ¼ c. creamed cottage cheese plus 1 tsp. oil, or 4 tsp. soy protein powder, available at health-food stores, plus 1 tsp. oil)

1/3 c. cooked brown rice (or bulgur, oatmeal, cornmeal, or whole wheat bread
½ c. creamed cottage cheese (or 1/3 c. dry curd cottage cheese plus 1 tsp. oil, or 6 oz. tofu)
1 Tbsp. grated or chopped vegetables (raw or steamed)

Mix together and serve.

Weight Feeding Guide — Cats
(daily nutrition requirement)

Cat's weight	Multiply recipe by:
5-6 lbs	2/3
7-8 lbs	3/4
9-10 lbs	1
11-12 lbs	1-1/3

The daily ration given above can be divided into two meals. It should be supplemented with the following powder and oil mix, or a commercial feline vitamin (which probably will not be vegetarian).

Cat Powder Mix

½ c. nutritional yeast
¼ c. bonemeal (or 3 Tbsp. dicalcium phosphate — made from rock
    and available in pet stores — as bonemeal really is ground up bones)
¼ c. kelp powder (can be partially replaced with alfalfa powder; both available at
    health-food stores)

Store mixture in a sealed jar on a dark shelf.

Cat Oil Mix

¾ c. vegetable oil
¼ c. cod-liver oil

20-40 IU vitamin E (to prevent
    spoilage)

Keep mixture refrigerated in a sealed bottle.

Daily Supplement for Cats

1 tsp. Cat Powder Mix
1 tsp. Cat Oil Mix

30-50 IU vitamin E (in addition to
    the oil mix)

Add the above ingredients to the food recipe as you are preparing it, or to
the meal when you serve it. (If serving two meals, divide supplements
accordingly.)

Except for the cod-liver oil, the above recipe is vegetarian. The grain
and vegetables can be varied to include your last night's leftovers. Try
whole wheat noodles or mashed potatoes. A little extra nutritional yeast
(no more than 1 tsp. per meal) sprinkled on top will add flavor that really
tempts many cats, as well as providing a natural flea repellent (the skin of
an animal who regularly eats nutritional yeast and garlic will not taste good
to fleas).

Leanne reports: "What's great is that we've been able to feed the cats
basically what we eat. Both are fatter, sleeker, and in much better health
than when we found them. We do give them dry commercial cat food now
and again. It is especially handy to have a supply in the food bowl if you're
going to be gone for a day."

Another determined vegetarian is getting her cats, who are accustomed
to tasty commercial pet treats and canned foods to make the switch. She's
trying Vege Burger®, a canned Loma Linda product which costs no more
than the KalKan® she had been buying.

As with dogs' menus, new items can be introduced gradually to the
feline diet. The Hanson family, with nine cats, has success mashing

garbanzos, creamed corn, peas, garlic, and nutritional yeast together and adding this mixture to the regular canned food in gradually increasing amounts, until the cats are eating one-third cat food, two-thirds vegies. Try cantaloupe on your cat for a treat. You'll be surprised! With patience, you can teach your feline companions to be more open-minded and greatly reduce their meat consumption.

We emphasize that for greater detail, or for the diet of a pet with special needs, consult Dr. Pitcairn's book. There is also an excellent vegan cookbook with a chapter on dog and cat food recipes. Entitled *The Cookbook for People Who Love Animals,* the book can be ordered from Gentle World, P.O. Box 1418, Umatilla, FL 32784.

Another helpful book is *Dogs & Cats Go Vegetarian* by Barbara Lynn Peden. The book outlines raw foods vegan diets for dogs and cats and even includes an order form for a synthetic taurine product (taurine is an amino acid cats require in their diets that is available naturally only in animal products).* Keep your eye out for additional recipes in vegetarian cookbooks. And remember, if we create a demand for more meatless pet foods, you can be sure that sooner or later, they will appear on the market.

It isn't what you do — it's why you do it. We need, therefore, to develop a greater sense of concern in our society not just for the health of the planet as it affects our well being, or the future health of our grandchildren. Rather, we need to learn how to care for and love living things for their own sake — and maybe, too, simply for the joy of caring and loving.

— David Hancocks

---

*The book and supplement can be ordered from Harbingers of a New Age, 06784 Canary Road, Westlake, OR 97493.

Commonly Asked Questions

If you're going to start talking about animal rights, you'll no doubt encounter some of these questions. We've presented here some responses that might help you address them.

1. Doesn't the Bible give us dominion over animals?

This is a country of religious freedom. Not all religions condone animal exploitation. Even among Christians and Jews there are varying interpretations of the Bible. Many people interpret 'dominion' as implying stewardship, not the right to exploit and, in fact, see exploitation as a deviation from a course directed by God that asks humans to be responsible for and to protect the other creatures of the Earth. God would perhaps be cruel to give animals such capacity to feel pain and fear while allowing humans the right to hurt them in all the ways we do.

2. How do we know animals feel pain?

A person asking this usually does not believe that animals don't feel pain. Ask them if they think their dog responds differently to a pat than to a kick. Just as we're pretty sure a baby — who can't say it in words — can feel pain, we can also read pain in the vocalizations and physical response of animals. Their nervous systems are much like our own, which is why researchers do studies of pain on animals.

3. Don't we have the right to use animals because we are more important than they are and because we have superior talents?

First, who are we more important to? All right, perhaps we are more important to other humans. Perhaps humans care more about humans than about other animals. But caring more for humans doesn't impute more intrinsic value to humans. I may care more for my children than for yours, but it doesn't make my children more important than yours in the overall scheme of things.

And what is superior? Some animals are faster, stronger, bigger, longer-lived and prettier than all human beings. And some animals are smarter, more creative, more independent and more rational than some human beings. Regardless — being superior, whether measured by intelligence or strength, is a dangerous criteria on which to dole out rights. That argument would allow one human being who is smarter than another the *right* to exploit the less intelligent. It also supports the philosophy behind "might makes right," which is an idea our own species has been battling against for centuries in our efforts to improve upon the roads of justice. If we don't like the philosophy when we apply it to human relations, then it is not a savory justification for our relations as they pertain to other animals.

Aren't you playing word games? Don't humans have greater value as a species than other animals because as a group we are more intelligent, more creative and more rational than animals?

The argument above is called The Greater Valuist Argument. Here is the counter to that argument: We crave rights because we feel pain and pleasure. If we didn't feel pain or pleasure, rights wouldn't matter to us. And what we feel is unique and separate for each individual. I can't feel your pain and you can't feel mine (we can feel empathy, but we can't actually, in reality, get inside of someone else and feel their feelings). Rights protect an individual's pursuit of pleasure and avoidance of pain so long as no one else is prevented from pursuing pleasure and avoiding pain. There is no line between the human species and others when it comes to an ability to feel pain and pleasure. To draw one on the basis of species is just as arbitrary as drawing one on the basis of IQ's above 150. Do we want to do that? Or do we want to say that pain is pain — no matter who feels it in what species — and begin to deal with those who suffer unjustly?

4. What about survival of the fittest — the strongest survive?

Again, this is a dangerous way to seat your ethics. You might be next. Are you going to adhere to this philosophy when you are older, permanently disabled, or physically weaker? At some point, it will come back to haunt you because there will always be someone or something fitter than you are, and with this argument, you are giving that being the right to exploit *you*.

5. Don't plants have feelings?

See our "Wrapup" section, where this is addressed.

6. Where do you draw the line? Do bugs have rights?

Not everyone agrees where to "draw the line." But we believe that if people start with an attitude that all beings — whether they are humans, dolphins, ants or trees — deserve respect, then, in general, the course we take will be more careful, more aware that all things are a part of the whole. Many of our contacts with insects are defensive and we may decide that we have the right to defend our health and safety when they are threatened. People have different answers to these questions. We don't know how an insect feels — so we do our best. On the other hand, we know that animals on farms, in laboratories, and in circuses do feel pain, and we can't sidestep this fact just because we can't draw a definite line between who suffers and who doesn't.

7. Aren't we naturally meat eaters? Other animals eat meat, why can't we?

We don't appear to need to eat meat, so why should we live on the lives and suffering of others? Anatomically, humans are more closely related to herbivores than to carnivores. Among characteristics we share with herbivores and *not* with carnivores are: the long length of our intestines, molar teeth for grinding, incisors, sucking liquids rather than lapping, full-body perspiration, alkaline instead of acidic saliva, and jaws that can move sideways for grinding. You won't find any of these attributes in a cat or a hyena, but check out a horse or a deer. It appears that human meat-eating developed primarily after most of our biological evolution, so our bodies do not require meat. Even in early hunter-gatherer societies, it is generally thought that hunting wasn't usually very successful, and that "gathering" (vegetable food, nuts, berries, tubers, etc.) provided for the majority of the diet.

Among the noblest in the land — though man may count himself the least — that man I honor and revere, who without favor, without fear, in the great city dares to stand, the friend of every friendless beast.

— Henry Wadsworth Longfellow

Another thing we often forget is that modern western culture is not the only successful lifestyle. In many cultures, eating meat is not a historical habit.

But even if we found that our very ancient ancestors did eat meat, we still know that biologically we don't need to eat meat. Vegetarianism is healthy, and we can make our choices based on ethics rather than old habits.

You do not settle whether an experiment is justified or not by merely showing that it is of some use. The distinction is not between useful and useless experiments, but between barbarous and civilized behaviour. Vivisection is a social evil because if it advances human knowledge it does so at the expense of human character.

— George Bernard Shaw

---

8. But is vegetarianism healthy?

Yes. In fact, if you read between the lines of most cancer and heart disease studies, the message is clear — don't eat meat. Usually the phrase is "decrease animal-fat intake." Sometimes they don't spell it out, but they mean meat. There are many studies favorably comparing vegetarians to meat eaters on incidence of colon cancer, breast cancer, heart disease, high blood pressure, osteoporosis, arteriosclerosis and strokes. The studies are in the medical journals, though the meat lobby prefers that you don't know about them. This also is a reminder to look at who sponsored the nutrition studies you grew up with that favored our four basic food groups (heavy on meat and dairy). A close look will show that many were sponsored by meat and dairy interests.

Nutrition is always controversial, but evidence abounds that vegetarians are healthy. You will find millions of vegetarians and vegans around you, including athletes and body builders, who have not withered away from lack of meat consumption.

9. Isn't it okay to use animals that are specifically bred for research, for furs, or to be eaten?

Would you say that if a human was born into slavery, then slavery is acceptable? No. We would object, knowing that that human was a feeling being with a desire for free will, and with much more potential than only to be a slave. How are animals any different in this respect? Animals bred for research, food and furs aren't unfeeling machines. They can still feel pain, they still have feelings. And, in fact, they often suffer in captivity from far worse conditions than other animals that were not born to those purposes. It is arrogant for us to so callously determine the purpose of another's existence.

10. *What if your child was dying? Wouldn't you feel differently about animal experimentation?*

Certainly you have a greater emotional investment in your child than in the dog in the cage. And likely you'd choose the child over the dog — just as you might choose to save your child over someone else's if they were both caught in a burning house. But from an objective point of view, the other child has as much right to be saved as does yours, and the dog has a right to his own life. Emotional preferences do not confer the right to inflict harm. Instead of getting mad at animal rights people, get mad at the medical profession for not exploring new ways of research that might take us out of this ghastly predicament.

11. *Don't animals benefit from research too?*

Most research on animals is not done for the animals' benefit, it is done for humans; if knowledge contributes to animal medicine, it is simply an afterthought. It is rather audacious to justify the subjugation of unconsenting animals to pain and confinement by saying "animals benefit too." Most importantly, the animals who are being sacrificed do not benefit. We don't believe in sacrificing one human to serve the interests of even one hundred others. And, in turn, it is not right that one group of animals live their lives in pain and imprisonment to be sacrificed in the name of research that might benefit another group — human or nonhuman.

12. **If an animal is going to be put to death in an animal shelter anyway, why not use him in research so his life isn't wasted?**

Euthanasia in a shelter that uses the injection method is quick and painless; the point is to relieve suffering. In a laboratory, a dog or cat may live for several years in a cage, subjected to experiment after experiment, pain, boredom and stress before he or she is finally "sacrificed." Which would you rather endure — a quick and painless death, or a lifetime of suffering? The use of pound animals in research is a betrayal of animals and a betrayal of public trust. Euthanasia is a horrible, but merciful, choice. Someday, animal rights and animal welfare movements will create a better choice. The animal's life is robbed in either a shelter or a laboratory, but in laboratories there is the added insult of suffering.

I'm not directly involved in publicly protesting these issues but it breaks my heart . . . I can't believe how people do those things to animals. On a personal level, I wouldn't buy a fur coat because there are other ways to keep warm.

— *Patti Reagan Davis*

---

13. **Why is euthanasia (death) of animals in animal shelters acceptable to animal rights people?**

First of all, euthanasia is not "accepted" by any animal rights person as an acceptable status quo. Animal rights and animal welfare people work hard to change conditions so that future generations of animals need not be abandoned and then put to death because of people who haven't taken responsibility for their animals. We work for a day when our whole attitude toward animals in society will change, and life will no longer be considered "throw away." In the meantime, the majority of pet animals born have no chance of finding a home. The alternatives for them are not nice. Abandoned, they may starve, suffer thirst and disease, be hit by a car, be abused, shot at, trapped, poisoned, freeze in winter, and live in terror. They don't usually survive for long, and it is a life domesticated animals are not prepared for. Those of us who have seen the abandoned animals' alternatives usually would choose the easier and more painless death by injection of barbiturates. There is no good answer, but the consideration is for what is best for the animal. There is no profit to shelter workers from this choice, as there is on a factory farm or in a research lab. All shelters should work for the day when no animal may be put into a no-win situation. The status quo is unacceptable, and if people in shelters aren't trying to change it through education and outreach, then they have no business being there.

14. *The animal rights position seems to be against medical progress.*

We are not against medical progress, but we are against ethical retardation. If medical progress negatively affects ethics, then it is not the right kind of progress. Even so, we believe medical progress can still be made by exploring other avenues. Some alternatives exist, including tissue and bacteria cultures, computer models, and prevention. It is interesting to note, for instance, that more progress was made against cancer by a public relations "no smoking" campaign than by all the years of research on smoking dogs. In any case, we have to keep in mind in all of our strivings that quantifiable progress, as in medicine, isn't the only kind of progress, nor the best for us. Even if we give up a little medical progress in exchange for progress in compassion and caring attitudes for other suffering beings, we gain in another way, and our world would be better and healthier all around.

15. *Regarding fur and leather — the animal is already dead; I didn't kill it, but I might as well wear it.*

First. Yes, the animal is already dead, but by buying this fur or leather garment you are creating "demand," and more animals will be killed to meet that demand.

Second. Even if your fur is an old one, wearing it advertises the "desirability" of fur. Others may follow your fashion taste and go out and buy a new one. Your message is that this is acceptable. It is *not* acceptable. It is a product and a symbol of suffering.

16. *I'll bet you animal rights people aren't consistent. Don't you wear leather?*

Most of us *don't*. We avoid leather, we avoid products that have been tested on animals, and we avoid products with animal ingredients. Even so, it has to be said that to be perfectly pure is almost impossible. In this society, animal products are so pervasive you will likely find inconsistencies in each of us. Even to drive on paved streets is to use a product of exploited animals, since the pavement has rendering plant products in it. But even if you find inconsistencies in an animal rights person, does this, in turn, change the facts of our argument? Factory farming, trapping and vivisection are cruel, and this remains true regardless of the habits of the person making the statement. Because someone might be inconsistent, does it mean you cannot consider the reasoning on your own?

17. *On the issue of hunting, won't the animals starve if they are not shot?*

This argument puts the hunter in the good-guy role. The hunter kills for the "good" of the animals. Well, it doesn't wash. Each year, via "game management" programs, the population of "game" animals is deliberately and artificially manipulated so that by the time hunting season rolls around, the population is high enough to need "culling." Some ways this is effected are: millions of acres of forest are burned and bulldozed to create grazing areas; predators and competing animals are not protected and often have bounties on them, which reduces the number of diseased or weak game animals that would be killed in a more natural environment; and hunting changes the male-female ratio. In other words, human management manipulates deer numbers so that there are enough to hunt; thus, in the end, hunting actually *contributes* to the problem of starvation among game animals.

18. **Shouldn't we worry first about endangered species?**

There's nothing wrong with putting your energy into helping an endangered part of our environment, but it's based on a different idea than what is behind the animal rights movement. The philosophy of animal rights does not place one species above another, we look at *individual* beings. An animal does not have to be endangered or exotic to be exploited or to suffer pain. There are millions of cats and dogs and cows, but the fact that they are numerous doesn't justify cruelty or abuse to individuals among them. By all means, work for endangered species; but don't, by your lifestyle and habits, work against other animals. Farm and lab animals suffer as much as do whales and seals, and their problems exist right here in our own backyard.

19. **Wouldn't many people lose their jobs if changes were made to accommodate animal rights?**

Complete change does not happen overnight, and society adjusts to gradual change, although some unfortunately do suffer. People who sold horse-drawn plows probably suffered when machinery became the fashion. The world always changes and economics should not be our sole determiner of decision making. Ending slavery was considered a hazardous economic step — yet could any of us today feel that slavery should have continued for economic reasons? And it was feared that women voting would have economic repercussions. Would any woman today like to give up her voting rights to safeguard our economy? Our goal is not to hurt people. Yes, we sympathize with those who might have to suffer changes, especially the small guy. (But today, those that make the biggest profits from animal exploitation are the big corporations owning factory farms and those putting 4 billion dollars into research each year.)

If we stop exploiting animals, many more opportunities may open up. Land will be freed. A business of alternative research may develop. And, very possibly, we will find ourselves more sensible to other global problems when our compassion and sense of fairness extends to the most vulnerable among us.

20. *How far do you want to go? Do you want to give animals the right to vote and to have free speech?*

Rights are based on our needs. If we didn't have a system of language, we wouldn't need free speech. Animals don't need to vote or have press freedom; but they do need to be able to turn around and to stretch, to avoid genetic and medical manipulation, and to socialize with their own kind. So let's talk about their legitimate and rightful needs realistically.

21. *Why should I even care about animals?*

We should care because all of us are responsible for what happens in the world. We should care because we understand the unfairness of oppression and know how easily it can be turned back on us. We should care because the changes in attitudes and habits we describe make this a better world for humans, too. We should care because the genuine big "T" truth of the matter is that we (that is, the entire planet) are all in this together. We're linked by the sun that evaporates the water that makes the cloud that makes the rain that feeds the seed that feeds the bird to make it sing in our ears. If we neglect the web, it will break and we will all lose. You may not care enough, or have enough extra energy to be active, but you can care enough not to contribute to the problems. And it's funny — if everyone cared at least that much, most of our human-made problems would disappear.

22. *Animals have my sympathy, but with all the people problems in the world, why don't you spend your energy addressing the people problems?*

Why do you assume we don't? Many animal rights people are active in many non-animal causes. Actually, the question is slightly insulting. Would you dare ask a person working for civil rights why she or he isn't working for the rights of senior citizens? Why tell anyone their cause isn't important? We quote a local activist by saying that "no one should have to stand in line for their rights." Those who are minorities and have felt the burden of oppression, fear and prejudice, arbitrariness and legal inequality, should know this better than most. You know what we mean; there is no excuse or justification for any individual, human or not, to suffer for these reasons. We all have to be responsible for what we contribute to. We all should scrutinize our attitudes. Humans hurt animals. Animals cannot speak for themselves. Thus humans must speak for them.

23. **Okay, I care. But I can't bear to look at gruesome pictures and listen to your terrible descriptions.**

Well, if you never look, how do you know that you aren't responsible for some of things you cringe at? You haven't the right to not look if you are contributing. That is, if we believe we are responsible for our actions — even those that are indirect. So if you buy meat and support research, you should look. And if you care so much — but it hurts you — think of how the animal hurts and just maybe, with knowledge, you can *help.*

24. **I can't stop eating meat. I like the taste.**

Not all ethical vegetarians gave up meat easily. But in weighing habit against conscience, conscience was considered the better leader. What if the habit was eating hamburgers, only you found out they were made from human babies? Would you break the habit? Of course. So too, an animal's right to avoid suffering, boredom, manipulation and death is more important than satisfying your tastebuds. You can show restraint even if you previously thought you couldn't. You do have power to follow your conscience. Give yourself credit for having that power. It's a way we can make our life choices mean something.

25. **You're overwhelming me. Diet, clothing, entertainment, attitudes. I believe you are right, but it's such a big problem — I can't handle so much overload.**

Just as the animal rights movement is not expecting an overnight transformation of the general public, you shouldn't necessarily expect yourself to know everything or do everything in one day. If you can and you want to, fine. Some people do, but many others evolve with a goal in mind — and that's great — after all, this is a piecemeal Peace Meal Diet book. Look at your life and see what you can change first. Get support from your friendly and sympathetic local animal rights activist. *And read this book* — it was written to address this question. When you do make changes, you'll discover what we've learned — every "sacrifice" is not a sacrifice, because you've gained so much in peace of mind, and in knowledge of your personal power. If you want to do more than live a cruelty-free lifestyle, become active. Tell your friends about what happens behind closed doors on farms and in labs. Join a local group; we've listed them in the part entitled "Animal Rights Organizations."

Also, enjoy your life; that's why we have senses and emotions. Don't become so obsessed with purity that you become a shut-in. That won't help animals, because no one will hear about what you now know. And stay healthy in mind. If you need a break from crusading (but not from lifestyle) allow yourself to take a break. It's a long haul, and burnout is common if you don't have some fun along the way.

So choose your level of activism and choose your pace, but make the change to cruelty-free living, because the pain is far worse for the animals than it is for you.

"I NEVER SHOULD'VE LISTENED TO THAT COWBOY WHO SAID 'WANT TO EARN A BUCK?' ".

Our Warm Thanks to the Following Businesses
for their Donations to this Book

Adventist Book Center

Bahn Thai Restaurant

C.W. Bodkins, Ltd.

Guido's Pizzeria

International Society for Krishna Consciousness

Kokeb Restaurant

Manna Mills

Mari-Don Healthway

Minglement

Morningtown Restaurant

Mother Nature's Natural Foods

Rainbow Grocery

Rama House Thai Restaurant

Sound Food Restaurant and Bakery

Vegetable Kingdom

Ways to Promote
Animal Rights On Your Own

Making your ideas visible will eventually make them less and less foreign to the general public. This list will provide some ideas as to how to advertise animal rights in everyday situations. It's full of easy-to-perform suggestions, yet serves an important purpose in helping to place the issue of animal rights before more and more people. It may be especially helpful to you if you find yourself unable to involve yourself wholeheartedly in group projects, but still wish to contribute to the cause.

1. PAWS sells "I WANT YOU FOR ANIMAL RIGHTS" T-shirts and bumper stickers. Call PAWS at 743-1884 for details.

2. Request your local library to obtain Peter Singer's book, *Animal Liberation*. Make repeated requests. Also request it at co-ops, bookstores, etc.

3. Each time you eat out at a restaurant, leave a note on your bill, i.e., "Thank you for your vegetarian selection!"

4. Write a letter, leave a note, or verbally ask at health-food stores for them to stock cosmetics from companies that don't experiment or contain any animal products. Ask if you can put a little label on the cruelty-free products designating them as such.

5. Read the newspapers and write a letter to the editor each time an animal rights-related article is presented.

6. Xerox animal rights flyers and post on bulletin boards at work, school, laundromats, etc.

7. When you send letters, write a message on the outside (e.g. "Animal rights are right.")

8. Copy Mart will copy on gumbacked paper ($1 for 10 sheets). Type up a sheet of slogans, copy them and cut them up for stickers which can be put on letters, etc.

9. Leave suggestions at cafeterias, fast food places, and other restaurants asking them to increase their vegetarian selection.

10. Send an animal rights/vegetarian rights questionnaire to your political representatives. Also, let your feelings be known to them on animal rights-related issues.

11. If you're in school, write a paper or do a speech on animal rights. Submit an article to your school newspaper. Suggest to instructors that the topic be up for instruction and perhaps ask in a speaker from PAWS. Videotapes, slide shows and books are available to borrow from PAWS.

12. Leave cards with an animal rights message in library books, phone books, and other places where people will find them.

13. Put a classified ad in a newspaper with an animal rights message.

14. Leave animal rights magazines and articles in laundromats, doctors' and dentists' offices, etc.

15. Give vegetarian cookbooks as gifts.

16. Throw vegetarian dinner parties, or cruelty-free cosmetic parties.

17. If you donate to an alumni association or a disease-research organization, specify that the donation not be used for animal experimentation.

Wrap Up

What's all this about Animal Rights? There are wars in Central America, people starving around the world, and the bomb waiting to fall from the sky. Why should we worry about Animal Rights? A local activist once wrote "no one should have to stand in line for their rights." We see Animal Rights as a part of the humane movement, not a separate or eccentric issue. We don't expect everyone to drop what they are doing currently and to funnel their energies into Animal Rights. But just as with other concerns — from Women's Rights to Ecology, from Gay Rights to Disarmament, whether you work directly for the issue or not — the choices you make in your personal life either support a philosophy or work against it.

The Unity of Creation: "*We need another and a wise and, perhaps, a more mystical concept of animals. We patronize them for their incompleteness, for their tragic fate of having taken form so far below ourselves. And therein we err, and greatly err. For the animal shall not be measured by man. In a world older and more complete than ours they move finished and complete, gifted with extensions of the senses we have lost or never attained, living by voices we shall never hear. They are not brethren, they are not underlings; they are other nations, caught with ourselves in the net of life and time, fellow prisoners of the splendour and travail of the earth.*"

— *The Outermost House*
by Henry Beston

The philosophy behind Animal Rights is that animals feel pleasure and feel pain, and just as we feel it would be wrong to cause suffering to one group of people so that another group might benefit, Animal Rights proponents believe it is wrong to cause animals to suffer in the name of human good. Causing suffering as a means does not create a worthy end. And the level of suffering these days cannot go on being ignored. We think of this philosophy as a basic part of the peace movement. It is a nonviolent approach that promotes respect and peace for all life.

Sometimes asked with complete sincerity, and often asked by meat-eaters looking for an excuse to punch holes in the Animal Rights/vegetarian philosophy, the question "What about plants, don't they have feelings too?" is posed to the ethical vegetarian. We do believe in reverence for all life, and though it is obvious to most of these people that animals feel physical pain in a way we know hurts, still we agree that those studies showing that plants have feelings should not be ignored. The vegetarian lifestyle causes less plant death than does that of a meat-eater when you consider the tremendous amount of vegetable matter a cow, or a pig, etc., must eat to make one pound of "meat." If you are worried about plants, then become a vegetarian. Also, it is unlikely that a plant, which has no means of running away, would ever have evolved a nervous system that reacts with the traditional pain to stimuli. Pain is usually a clue for an animal to run away, or to act differently — a useless adaptation for a plant, which has no motility. So the fact that plants may have feelings should not divert our attention from our efforts to address animal suffering.

We do the best that we can. We do not have to eat meat, and especially, we do not have to support industries that survive by the debasement and disregard of the needs of the beings they use. It is time to look up from our calculator of convenience and to begin a new measure of progress — ethical progress. And while we're working to bring peace to our human family throughout the world by rejection of institutionalized violence and economic warfare, let us broaden the scope of our principles to include respect and care for nonhuman animals. Nonhuman animals share many of our needs; they cry in pain and fear, but they cannot speak for themselves.

We are not speaking of a little suffering by a few beings. As we bring this book to a close, we present to you these numbers to consider: Thirteen million companion animals are euthanized in America's animal shelters each year, most left there by their owners. Each year, seventy million animals die in American research laboratories. More than thirteen million animals annually are caught in steel-jaw leghold traps — dogs, cats, rabbits, beavers, squirrels, birds. And, according to the United States Department of Agriculture, every day, eleven million animals are slaughtered in this country for our consumption... two hundred every second... four billion animals a year...

National Animal-Related Organizations

American Humane, P.O. Box 1266, Denver, CO 80201

Animalines, 33 Millwood, Mill Valley, CA 94941, (415) 381-0838

Animal Legal Defense Fund, 333 Market Street, 23 fl., San Francisco, CA 94105.

Animals' Defender, 51 Harley Street, London, W1N-1696.

American Vegan Society, 501 Old Harding Highway, Malaga, NY 08328; (609) 694-2887.

Animal Protection Institute (API), P.O. Box 22505, Sacramento, CA 95822.

Beauty Without Cruelty, 175 W. 12th Street, New York, NY 10011.

Buddhists Concern for Animals, 300 Page Street, San Francisco, CA 94102.

Farm Animal Reform Movement, Box 70123, Washington, D.C. 20088.

The Fund for Animals, Inc., 12548 Venture Blvd., Suite 141, Studio City, CA 91604.

Humans Against Rabbit Exploitation (HARE), P.O. Box 1351, State College, PA 16804.

Humane Society of the United States, 2100 L. Street N.W., Washington, D.C. 20037.

International Society for Animal Rights, Inc., 421 S. State St., Clarks Summit, PA 18411.

National Association for the Advancement of Humane Education (NAAHE), Division of HSUS, Box 362, East Haddam, CT 06423.

National Alliance for Animal Legislation, P.O. Box 77012, Washington, D.C. 20013.

People for the Ethical Treatment of Animals (PETA), Box 42516, Washington, D.C. 20015.

Society for Animal Protective Legislation, P.O. Box 3719, Georgetown Station, Washington, D.C. 20007.

United Action for Animals, 205 E. 42nd St., New York, NY 10017.

Vegetarian Information Service, Box 5888, Bethesda, MD 20814; (301) 530-1737.

World Society for the Protection of Animals, P.O. Box 190, Boston, MA 02130.

The American Anti-Vivisection Society, Suite 204, Noble Plaza, 801 Old York Road, Jenkintown, PA 19046.

The National Anti-Vivisection Society, 100 E. Ohio St., Chicago, IL 60611.

Defenders of Wildlife, 1244 Nineteenth St. N.W., Washington, D.C. 20036.

Wildlife Rehabilitation Council, P.O. Box 3007, Walnut Creek, CA 94598.

Trans-Species Unlimited, P.O. Box 1351, State College, PA 16804

Local Animal-Related Organizations

Progressive Animal Welfare Society (PAWS) Animal Rights Action Committee (ARAC), P.O. Box 1037, Lynnwood, WA 98046; (206) 743-3845. Holds monthly meetings in Seattle and addresses wide spectrum of animal-rights issues such as farm animals, laboratory experimentation on animals, furs, rodeos, hunting, etc. PAWS also runs an animal shelter and wildlife clinic based in Lynnwood.

University of Washington Students for Animal Rights, University of Washington, HUB, Room 207, Seattle, WA 98195. Closely affiliates with actions undertaken by ARAC.

ARK Foundation, P.O. Box 45801, Seattle, WA 98105. Accepts tax-deductible donations and channels them to animal-rights and animal-welfare groups.

Greenpeace, 4649 Sunnyside N., Seattle, WA 98103. Emphasis on endangered species and the ecology. Spearheads campaigns against whaling and seal hunts. Believes in non-violent, direct action.

MR PAC (Modern Research Political Action Committee), 168 Galer St., Seattle, WA 98109. Main concern is legislative reform of abusive procedures performed on animals in research institutions.

PETA (People for the Ethical Treatment of Animals), (206) 392-9338. Local branch of national organization which actively addresses animal rights issues.

Further Reading
Animal Rights and Vegetarian Books and Periodicals

"ANIMALS AGENDA, A Journal of Animal Liberation;" a journal to promote communication and cooperation within the animal welfare/rights/liberation movement; Doug Moss, ed. P.O. Box 5234, Westport, CT 06880: Animal Rights Network.

Animal Factories by Jim Mason and Peter Singer. New York: Crown Publishers, 1980.

Animal Liberation: A New Ethics for Our Treatment of Animals by Peter Singer. New York: Avon Books, 1975.

Animal Rights and Human Obligations; Tom Regan and Peter Singer, eds. Englewood Cliffs, NJ: Prentice-Hall, 1976.

Animals, Men and Morals: An Enquiry Into the Maltreatment of Non-Humans; Stanley and Roslind Godlovitch, and John Harris, eds. New York: Taplinger Publishing, 1972.

Animals' Rights by Henry S. Salt. Clarks Summit, PA: Society for Animal Rights, 1980.

All That Dwell Therein by Tom Regan. Berkeley: University of California Press, 1982.

The Case for Animal Rights by Tom Regan. Berkeley: University of California Press, 1983.

Facts About Furs by Greta Nilsson and others. Washington, D.C.: Animal Welfare Institute, 1980.

Man Kind? Our Incredible War on Wildlife by Cleveland Amory. New York: Harper and Row, 1974.

Painful Experiments on Animals by Dallas Pratt. New York: Argus Archives, 1976.

Alternatives to Pain in Experiments on Animals by Dallas Pratt. New York: Argus Archives, 1980.

Physical and Mental Suffering of Experimental Animals by Jeff Diner. Washington, D.C. 20007: Animal Welfare Institute, Box 3650, 1979.

The Plague Dogs (fiction) by Richard Adams. New York: Knopf, 1978.

Slaughter of the Innocent by Hans Ruesch. New York: Bantam Books, 1978.

Traps & Trapping, Furs & Fashion, New York 10017: Argus Archives, 228 E. 49th St., 1977.

Vegetarianism — A Way of Life by Dudley Giehl. New York: Harper and Row, 1979.

Vegetarian Sourcebook: Nutrition, Ecology and Ethics of a Natural Foods Diet by Vic S. Sussman. Emmaus, PA: Rodale Press, 1978.

"Vegetarian Times;" Paul Obis, ed. New York 10017: Vegetarian Life and Times, 41 East 42nd Street, Suite 921.

Cookbooks

Benjamin, Alice and Corrigan, Harriett. *Cooking with Conscience: A Book for People Concerned About World Hunger.* New York: Seabury Press, 1978.

Black Hills Health & Education Center. *Cooking with Natural Foods, 6th edition.* Ellendale, N.D.: Trinity Press, 1984.

Brown, Edward Espe. *Tassajara Cooking.* Berkeley: Shambhala, 1973.

Bruell, Stephany. *Mother Morgan's Vegetarian Cookbook.* Seattle: By Mother Morgan's, 431-15th East, n.d.

Krsna Devi, Dasi, and Sama Devi, Dasi, comps. *The Hare Krsna Cookbook.* New York: The Bhaktivedanta Book Trust, 1973.

Gentle World. *The Cookbook for People Who Love Animals, 3rd edition.* Umatilla, FL: 1986.

Goldbeck, Nikki and David. *The Supermarket Handbook.* New York: Signet, 1973.

Hagler, Louise, ed. *The Farm Vegetarian Cookbook.* Summertown, TN: Book Publishing Co., 1975.

Hagler, Louise. *Tofu Cookery.* Summertown, TN: Book Publishing Co., 1983.

Hoshijo, Kathy. *Kathy Cooks Naturally.* New York: Bantam Books, 1982.

Island Spring. *Tofu Madness.* Vashon, WA: By Island Spring, P.O. Box 747, 1978.

Katzen, Mollie, ed. and comp. *The Moosewood Cookbook: Recipes from Moosewood Restaurant, Ithaca, New York.* Berkeley: Ten Speed Press, 1977.

Landgrebe, Gary. *Tofu Goes West.* Palo Alto, CA: Fresh Press, 1978.

Lappe, Frances Moore. *Diet for a Small Planet: 10th Anniversary Edition.* New York: Ballantine Books, 1982.

Pitcairn, Richard H., and Pitcairn, Susan Hubble. *Dr. Pitcairn's Complete Guide to Natural Health for Dogs and Cats.* Emmaus, PA: Rodale Press, 1982.

Robertson, Laurel; Flinders, Carol; and Godfrey, Bronwen. *Laurel's Kitchen: A Handbook for Vegetarian Cookery and Nutrition.* New York: Nilgiri Press, 1976.

Thomas, Anna. *The Vegetarian Epicure.* New York: Knopf, 1972.

A Note to Other Cities

As far as we know, *The Seattle Peace Meal Diet* is the first book of its kind — but we hope it's not the last. One reason for writing this book was to encourage animal groups in other cities to do the same. Public education on animal suffering and the cruelty-free alternatives is lacking in most locales. Our movement will make more headway when we can point out the cruelty-free alternatives to the public in an unscattered, accessible and positive manner.

We encourage you to use this book as a guide. Change the specifics to fit your locale. Along with your own improvements, you may borrow ideas, chapters, and text from *The Seattle Peace Meal Diet*.

While we are glad to offer our format, we offer it only to those groups and people who intend to use the profits for animal rights and animal welfare. Write us for permission. We'll give it to you, as well as any other tips regarding format, funding, and information gathering that might be of assistance.

So here's to you — Baltimore, Denver, Minneapolis and all of the other cities — that together we might someday really achieve a lifestyle of peace that recognizes the sanctity of all life on our planet.